GEOLOGICAL FILMMAKING

Sasha Litvintseva

The **MEDIA : ART : WRITE : NOW** series mobilises the medium of writing as a mode of critical enquiry and aesthetic expression. Its books capture the most original developments in technology-based arts and other forms of creative media: AI and computational arts, gaming, digital and post-digital productions, soft and wet media, interactive and participative arts, open platforms, photography, photomedia and, last but not least, amateur media practice. They convey the urgency of the project via their style, length and mode of engagement. In both length and tone, they sit somewhere between an extended essay and a monograph.

Series Editor: Joanna Zylinska

GEOLOGICAL FILMMAKING

Sasha Litvintseva

○
OPEN HUMANITIES PRESS

London 2022

First edition published by Open Humanities Press 2022
Copyright © 2022 Sasha Litvintseva

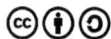

Freely available at:
http://openhumanitiespress.org/books/titles/geological-filmmaking/

This is an open access book, licensed under Creative Commons By Attribution Share Alike license. Under this license, authors allow anyone to download, reuse, reprint, modify, distribute, and/or copy their work so long as the authors and source are cited and resulting derivative works are licensed under the same or similar license. No permission is required from the authors or the publisher. Statutory fair use and other rights are in no way affected by the above. Read more about the license at creativecommons.org/licenses/by-sa/4.0

Cover Art, figures, and other media included with this book may be under different copyright restrictions.

Print ISBN 978-1-78542-110-5
PDF ISBN 978-1-78542-109-9

OPEN HUMANITIES PRESS

Open Humanities Press is an international, scholar-led open access publishing collective whose mission is to make leading works of contemporary critical thought freely available worldwide.
More at http://openhumanitiespress.org/

Contents

Acknowledgements   7

Preface: Nature's Cultural Hall   11

1. Grounding   23
   Filmmaking   23
   The Geological   35
   Geological Time and Film Time   43

2. Perception: Asbestos   53
   On the Relationality of (In)Visibility   55
   Asbestos: Toxic and Haptic   65
   Asbestos: Inside and Outside   72
   Asbestos Time: Material Debt and Unintended Consequences   93

3. Depiction: Sinkholes   103
   Nature Represents Itself?   105
   Sinkholes: Life and Nonlife, Surface and Depth   111
   On Dimensionality   124
   The Sinkhole Image   131

Works Cited   147

Acknowledgements

My immense gratitude to Joanna Zylinska, who saw this project through from the start and whose exacting eye taught me rigour, for her invitation to publish in the series. And also to Rachel Moore who supported and inspired the project's growth throughout.

I am indebted to my collaborators and dear friends Graeme Arnfield and Daniel Mann. Without our shared obsessions this project would have looked very different. Your approaches to filmmaking will always be incredibly meaningful to have intersected with.

A big thanks to many other friends for reading, supporting, sharing inspiration and showing solidarity along the way, in particular Solveig Suess, Peter Rees, Scott Wark, Annie Goh, Roberto Mozzachiodi, Mihaela Brebenel, Nikolaus Perneczky, Ifor Duncan and Isabel Mallet.

Thank you to my dear colleagues at the Film department at Queen Mary University of London. In particular to Janet Harbord, who was one of the last to read the material in this form, and to whom I am indebted in so many ways.

Acknowledgements

I am grateful to all the many people who have invited me to speak about the project at its various stages over the years, particularly to Anastasia Kubrak and Lukas Brasiskis, whose invitations encouraged me to distill the coherency of the project as a whole.

Thank you to the editors of the special issues of Environmental Humanities and Transformations journals, in which some of the ideas present here have appeared in different forms, for their generous engagement with my work.

My gratitude to the many people who have screened and exhibited the films, creating opportunities to experience, frame, question and discuss them in new ways; and thank you also to the amazing artists and filmmakers concerned with these themes who I met along the way.

I further want to acknowledge my debt to the women theorists whose thinking is the bedrock for the sedimentation of mine: Karen Barad, Kathryn Yusoff, Elizabeth A. Povinelli, Susan Schuppli, Donna Haraway, Astrida Neimanis. Without the positions you established I could not have built mine.

Finally and most of all I want to thank my partner Beny Wagner for being a source of unbounded inspiration, unwavering support and immeasurable zest for life. You are forever my target audience.

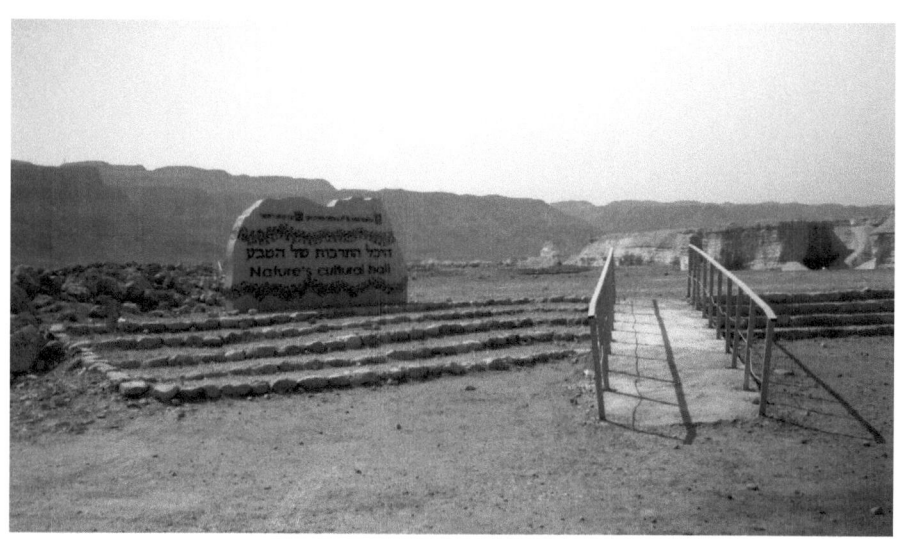

Fig 1. Still from *Salarium* (2017), Sasha Litvintseva and Daniel Mann.

Preface

Nature's Cultural Hall

'Nature's cultural hall' reads a solitary sign in an arid desert landscape. A mountain range obscures the horizon and the sky is a cloudless milky haze. My camera is on a tripod capturing this scene, while the rental car idling behind me blasts the air-conditioning. Over the last three days I have calculated that I can keep the camera rolling for exactly ninety seconds before it overheats, shuts down and corrupts the file. The sun blinds me as I remove my sunglasses to set the exposure on the camera. Even within these ninety-second intervals the scorching sun dehydrates my body and burns my skin. To the naked eye this landscape does not betray any visible signs of what we tend to call life; without the slightest movement, the shot that emerges from this moment will be practically indistinguishable from a photograph. By now I've learned to sense when to end the shot without having to rely on the camera's clock. I run back to the car to cool the camera and myself before we can once again take another shot.

We are in the Judean desert just off the Dead Sea shore. It is late July and the temperature is 48 degrees

Celsius. In July, it never drops below body temperature. Even in the middle of the night, it stays in the high thirties, and soon after the sun comes up, it is already in the upper forties. The sun here is in such excess that it obliterates its harnessing as a precious tourist commodity. In the extreme heat this tourist area is deserted, and my collaborator and I are able to park and shoot anywhere without obstruction. We have come here to make a film about the sinkholes that have been ravaging the Dead Sea coastline over the last forty years. The sinkholes are caused by anthropogenic interventions into the hydrogeophysics of the area, where the over-extraction of minerals and the diversion of water from River Jordan to irrigate desert orchards has lowered the sea level, leading to the creation of cavities under the surface of the earth. As we film just off the side of the road, there is a latent fear that the ground might collapse and swallow us, the camera or even the car. When we encounter the sign reading 'Nature's cultural hall', both in English and Hebrew, it comes across as an unauthored pun describing this moment back to us with deadpan precision.

There is a seeming contradiction in this sign that cannot quite be resolved. The sign has a strange way of creating a proximity between nature and culture so that they merge into one, while simultaneously keeping their definitions intact and at a distance. The contradiction that is held in balance by this sign becomes a useful metaphor for the irresolvable contradictions involved in trying to read the ways in which different human and nonhuman processes that occur on incommensurate scales and temporalities are intertwined. This book attempts to theorise points of exchange between many such processes, using 'the geological' and 'the filmic' as prisms. Both my own experience in this desert and the resulting images emerge out of the intersection of several human and nonhuman processes, and are themselves not without contradiction. As I document the ecological devastation, rooted in a multitude of political and economic causes, my presence there is also powered by equally destructive forces: I arrived at the desert by a budget flight and am burning lots of petrol to keep myself and the camera cool. The camera I use is made from minerals, metals, plastics and chemicals, some of which were formed in the crust of the earth billions of years ago and extracted from it at high environmental cost. Still, this project is driven by a belief that this aesthetic intervention could make a contribution towards a future where every step forward does not entail two steps back.

As I study the image of the sign in the desert, I keep returning to the ramp placed to the right of the sign. The ramp appears to provide accessibility to visitors who would not be able to climb the five shallow steps. Having looked at this image for hours, I begin to wonder why the steps were installed in the first place: there is no perceptible incline in the piece of land the steps are on. The ramp is an intervention into the landscape to mitigate a previous unnecessary intervention. My project takes place in the context of widespread ecological collapse and is in part invested in considering what a 'positive intervention' could mean given that we are living in a world that has seemingly been pushed to the brink *through* human intervention. It responds to our current moment, defined by the irreversible changes made to the geophysics of the earth by human influence, depletion of natural resources and an increase in the condensation of carbon dioxide and other greenhouse gases in the atmosphere, due to the burning of fossil fuels and deforestation. This increase in greenhouse gases is one of the symptoms of what has become known as anthropogenic climate change, as evidenced in the rising temperatures, frequent draughts, cyclones, forest fires, crop failures and the melting of mountain glaciers and polar ice caps in different parts of the globe. Carbon dioxide is also reacting with ocean waters, acidifying them and thus destroying marine ecosystems in a process named the Sixth Great Extinction, a mass extinction event that includes the rapid loss of biodiversity on land.

Many readers today would most likely find the account of the ecological situation presented above fairly uncontroversial, yet our knowledge of the facts presented does not itself pave the way forward. As Amitav Ghosh argues, despite there being no lack of factual information about the ecological crisis, our relative passivity with regard to climate change also entails a crisis of the imagination, rooted in our inability to grasp the scope and implications of said crisis. Ghosh stresses the pressing necessity of cultural production that would be able to grapple with the 'forces of unthinkable magnitude that create unbearably intimate connections over vast gaps in time and space' (2016, 63), and suggests that the current failure of much of contemporary cultural production to reckon with the perceptually elusive aspects of the ecological crisis 'will have to be counted as an aspect of the broader imaginative and cultural failure that lies at the heart of the climate crisis' (8). The ecological crisis, as well as its causes and potential responses to it, all take shape in the cultural imagination largely through mediation. The elements of this crisis are too dispersed to be experienced by any one person in their totality, although specific cases of extreme weather events and fires are becoming increasingly prevalent – significantly so in the few years I have been working on this project.

Even though some news outlets are working on improving their visual language around the crisis, as seen in *The Guardian*'s editorial on the change to their visual policy around the environmental catastrophe, where they promise 'to be using fewer polar bears and more people' (Shields 2019), evidential photography can only ever portray an isolated symptom of the crisis rather than its relationality and causality. Regardless of the shift in empathic response from endangered species stranded on melting icebergs to people stranded in their burning homes, such images fall short of being able to depict those aspects of the crisis that most challenge our imaginative capacities: its vast scale and the inextricable web of interconnected causes and agencies, both human and nonhuman, that define that crisis.

In broader mainstream culture the themes of extinction and ecological collapse find their voice primarily in apocalyptic blockbuster cinema. The ubiquity of the narrative forms inherited from modernity, from the bourgeois novel to the narrative fiction film, makes us crave an ecological catastrophe narrative with a resolution, be it trust in an impending technological fix or even resignation to an impending apocalypse. Narratives driven by the arc of 'problem, climax and resolution' are not up to the task of narrating a crisis that will have no easy solution or contained finality. The very necessity of a human protagonist (who invariably emerges triumphant at the end) to drive a plot of a feature narrative film, together with the familiarity of the Hollywood style of cinematography and editing (all of which scream business-as-usual) foreclose the possibility of contemplating the presence of nonhuman agencies or the prospect of radical change. Such narratives also preclude political mobilisation as they make the future seem predetermined: no action is necessary when the future is guaranteed, at least for the protagonists.

The perceptual is political. As Sean Cubitt argues, the political question of building an alliance of humans and nonhumans, and of avoiding environmental catastrophe, will ultimately have to be an aesthetic question. Aesthetics is understood here as 'concerning both perception (the root meaning of *aesthesis*) and art, the techniques of mediation and communication in which we construe our relations with one another and the world' (2017, 15). Neither economic nor technological fixes would suffice, as both are part of the machinery that perpetuates the crisis, and politics will only be effective 'if there is a radical change in how we conceive of and pursue politics' (15). Such change in turn could only arise through a remaking of 'aesthetic principles, that is, by remaking communications' (151). The aesthetic realm here becomes a ground upon which to imagine and therefore work towards a future: a politics that 'looks toward the unimaginable as an aesthetic category, the unimaginable good life for human, natural, and technological phyla in their once and future interdependence' (188). The political commitment, and the conceptual and practical challenge driving this project, lie in the development of modes of mediatic creative practice that stage an encounter between the human, the nonhuman and the technological as interdependent co-creators of the media artefact in question (film), as well as of the world and the future as such.

A foundational aesthetic problem of the ecological crisis is that our direct perceptual experience of it is limited by the fact that many of its material factors, such as greenhouse gas emissions or nuclear radiation, are both invisible to us and occur on a temporal scale that far exceeds human lifespans. This perceptual disjuncture makes it difficult to imagine not only the future but also the very present. How do we get our bearings among events occurring simultaneously on temporal and spatial micro- and macro-scales and how do we come to see geophysical phenomena as both planetary and situated? How do we understand humans as both material bodies and situated beings forming part of specific political and environmental arrangements, as both producers and products of ecological processes? *Geological Filmmaking* addresses these questions by way of two specific case studies, which involve an attempt to think through the making of two films.

The case studies are preceded and framed by chapter one, which provides a grounding for engaging with these questions. The chapter sets up some key methodological points in relation to filmmaking through engaging with a number of filmmaker-theorists, as well as unfolding some key aspects of what I call 'geological filmmaking' as both a concept and a methodology. It also reflects on the way 'the geological' has been used in philosophy – and the way it will be used in this book. Finally, it sets up multifaceted links between the geological and film across the material and temporal dimensions. It is upon the foundation of these links between the geological and *all* cinematic images that my investigation into specific cinematic forms builds.

The first of my questions tackles the perceptual problem: how to grapple with ecological phenomena that are imperceptible to both the human sensorium and technological perceptual prostheses. In chapter two I explore this question through the prism of asbestos: a mineral which, when airborne, is toxic and invisible both to the human eye and to optical apparatuses. In this chapter, and in the making of its accompanying film *Asbestos* (2016), I seek to find what can be made intelligible in attempting to engage with asbestos through the optical medium of film. One of the reasons for choosing asbestos as my subject is that it represents an iconic episode in the nonlinear history of industrial progress, with an almost total (but crucially, not full) reversal of its extraction and use after the unintended consequences of its toxicity came to light. The chapter ends by addressing what lessons the history and temporality of asbestos have to offer us in confronting the unfolding present of the ecological crisis more broadly.

Invisibility, however, is not the only aesthetic challenge presented by the crisis, as the question is not just *whether* this crisis is visible but also *how* it is mediated. The way that the environment is understood, represented and quantified socially and historically is as much implicated in the processes of earth-shaping as are the material processes of depletion, extraction, deforestation and toxification. As Jason W. Moore puts it: 'power, production, and perception entwine' (2015, 3). From the point of view of making depictions of the environment, the question of *how* is both an ethical and a formal one. According to avant-garde filmmaker Maya Deren, these are always and already one: 'the esthetic problem of form is, essentially, and simultaneously, a moral problem' as 'the form of the work of art is the physical manifestation of its moral structure' (2008, 85). My own philosophy of filmmaking is aligned with Deren's in more than one way, but this point is crucial. It is not possible to have an ethical approach to depicting or mediating the ecological crisis while using aesthetic tools and formal language that had been defined by a culture that caused it. The question of form is not trivial, and part of the practice of geological filmmaking consists in developing formal modes in response to the specificity of the subject matter of each film. In chapter three I thus examine the ethics and politics of depiction further through a critique of representationalist image-making, and explore formal alternatives through the case study of making a film, *Salarium* (2017), which engages with the sinkholes decimating the Dead Sea shore. I address the role of the occupation of the West Bank in the appearance of the sinkholes, the role of the sinkholes as agential producers of the changing landscape and the role of images in our understanding of both, as well as in their very unfolding.

These two latter chapters have been revised over a number of years but were originally written in parallel with the making of the two films. Both open with setting up a conceptual or theoretical problem, which I then address through practical filmmaking, with the latter parts of the chapter reflecting on and theorising the problem further. One way to encounter this book and its accompanying films is to watch the two films in relation to reading the respective chapters – two and three. However, both the films and the book can operate (and in the case of the films – have been operating) in a standalone manner and can therefore be encountered in any order.

The focus on the nonhuman affinity of the geological and the technological in chapter one, and the commitment to decentring the human in the entire project, do not mean that the human is ever absent from the field of either the aesthetic or the material processes under discussion. The vagaries of human perception, the vulnerability of human flesh and the temporality of socio-economic rhythms are inextricably connected with the films themselves and with their subjects, and thus are inextricable from the discussion of the ecological crisis or its mediation. As Cubitt emphatically puts it, 'the iron in our blood, the salt in our tears, tie us as deeply to our tools and planet as to one another, and we will never reach one another until we reach, and reach through, the nonhuman' (2017, 188), the nonhuman here being both planetary and technological. We are in the geological just as it is in us. We are in film just as it is in us.

CHAPTER I

Grounding

Filmmaking

Glorious volcano! I have never seen expressions comparable to yours. The conflagration had covered everything with the same colorless color, grey, dull, dead. In front of one's very eyes, every leaf on every tree passed through all the colors of autumn until, cracked, twisted and scorched, they fell into the fiery blasts. … Two hundred meters away, fiery rapids surged from an almost circular crevice and rushed down the slope to form a river as red as ripe cherries and as large as the Seine at Rouen. The vapor covered the sky with a porcelain whiteness. Little gusts of fetid, angry wind raised eddies of ash which fluttered just above the ground, strange seagulls living at the edge of the gigantic conflagration.
(Epstein 2012a, 288-90)

The epigraph features a description by filmmaker and critic Jean Epstein of an eruption of Mount Etna, which he had gone to film in 1923. The cadence of his writing, the choice of words and metaphors were, I would argue, driven by an attempt to put to paper the awe experienced in the face of geological immensity and geological change. Epstein resorts to metaphor in practically every sentence – lava becomes ripe cherries, sky becomes porcelain, ashes become seagulls – because there are not enough adjectives and not enough shared language between him and his readers to verbalise the singular event of a volcanic eruption that none of them had witnessed before. Perhaps most telling is the temporal metaphor that portrays leaves as going through an entire season within moments, because one of the most striking aspects of a volcanic eruption is its condensation of time. It is one of the most notable examples of geological time erupting out of the supposed imponderability of deep time and into the immediacy of the present. A volcanic eruption is the creation of the earth played as a time-lapse film: the elemental materials of the earth are melted down to their molecular subparts in the furnaces of its depths, bursting forth as liquid lava to cool into geological formations. A volcano is a testament to the impermanence of geological forms, as even the most majestic or iconic of mountains are but momentary solidifications of form in the ongoing circulation of material. With this in mind, let us consider the following quote in which Epstein describes the medium of film:

> The cinematograph shows us that form is only one unsettled state of a fundamentally mobile condition, and that movement, being universal and variably variable, makes every form inconstant, inconsistent, fluid. Solids suddenly find their supremacy threatened; they are but one particular genre of appearances within systems of ordinary experience on a human scale, which are either in constant motion or only slightly and uniformly varying. Fluidity – the reality of the cinematographic experience – is also the reality of a scientific outlook, which sees in every substance a gaseous structure. (Epstein 2012b, 322)

Like a volcano, Epstein sees cinema as a system engaged in the melting down and reconstitution of forms within the ongoing flows of movement. In the universal flows of change, matter is to geology what image is to film. Or, in other words, the geological might be defined as matter and process, and film, in turn, as image and movement. Film, or, as it is otherwise known, moving image, is a medium of movement, 'a technology that translates image, perception, consciousness and matter into movement' (Valiaho 2010, 6). And it is through movement that it is most closely connected to perception and consciousness. As Ute Holl outlines, visual perception of movement is separate from the perception of form. The perception of movement is processed by its own physiological process called oscillopsia. Experiments have shown that this process operates in the same way when seeing movement in film as in a three-dimensional environment. As Holl elaborates, 'since the experience of movement in the cinema can thus not be distinguished from the experience of real movement – while the depiction of spaces, forms, or shapes ... can be distinguished from their physical reality without any trouble – then seeing in the cinema is a more complex perceptual experience that can be grasped by the concept of representation' (2017, 41). The movement experienced in film 'is not represented, but presented' (41). It is through movement that film is able to *presence* entities and flows outside of our direct experience; it is through movement that it is able to enter our nervous systems and shape our perceptual frameworks. In Epstein's words, cinema is 'a domain of movement [wherein] form is not retained' (2012b, 324). It is precisely through this quality that cinema is able to engage with the transformations of form within the geological and turn them into a perceptual experience.

Epstein's contemporary, fellow filmmaker theorist and key figure in early French cinema Germaine Dulac, had also written about the eruption of Mount Etna, comparing it directly to the essence of cinema: 'lava and fire, a tempest expiring in a whirlwind of elements. ... The contest of blacks and whites, each wishing to dominate the other: *the cinégraphie of light*' (original emphasis; 1988, 327). Dulac too sees cinema from the point of view of a whirlwind of elements: light and dark, image and form, duration and movement, perception and consciousness are all exploded into their 'gaseous' or liquid elemental forms and reconstructed anew in cinema.

Her theoretical writings on film return time and again to film's privileged relationship to the nonhuman world and its ability to reveal previously unimaginable aspects of existence. She describes cinema as possessing 'an eye wide open on life, an eye more powerful than our own and which sees things we cannot see' (2018, 39). This is something that is also echoed in Epstein's thinking as he writes, 'if we wish to understand how an animal, a plant or a stone can inspire respect, fear and horror, those three most sacred sentiments, I think we must watch them on the screen, living their mysterious, silent lives, alien to the human sensibility' (Epstein 1981, 22). To Epstein, the camera eye is in its essence nonhuman; it is unburdened by the knowledge of the meaning of the objects it captures. It is for this reason that it is able to not only represent but also reveal the world of nonhuman agency. Dulac takes this thinking further to differentiate between such a capacity of the medium itself and the modes of filmmaking that do or do not exercise the medium to its full capacity. She calls for filmmaking that she terms 'pure cinema', which would go 'in search of emotion beyond the limits of the human, to ... the invisible, the imponderable' (2018, 47).

A generation later, in 1940s USA, and with studio-produced narrative fiction film even more firmly established, Maya Deren continues with the exploration of the unique powers of the cinematic medium to grapple with complex natural and technological phenomena – and with their perceptual ramifications. She undertakes this work across both her writings and filmmaking, where she searches for alternative forms she did not see being produced in the mainstream cinema of the time. She too sees the medium to have 'capacity for animating the ostensibly inanimate, for re-relating the ostensibly immobile' and to be 'especially equipped' for relating experiences that reveal the nonhuman world 'as an active, creative force' (Deren 2008, 32). She argues that these capacities of film are properly 'accomplished only when the elements, whatever their original context, are related according to the special character of the instrument of film itself – the camera and the editing – so that the reality which emerges is a new one – one which only film can achieve and which could not be accomplished by the exercise of any other instrument' (89). In this sense too film *presents* rather than represents as, when used to its full capacity as 'both a space art and a time art' (94), it creates entirely new realities, in ways unrelated to the actuality or stagedness of the events depicted. The power of the medium of film lies in its ability to generate new arrangements of space and time, to calibrate rhythms between human and nonhuman, to presence the imponderable. It is in this 'medium specific' sense that I am using the word 'film' throughout this book, rather than as a way of differentiating between analogue and digital moving images, or between fictional and nonfictional approaches. 'Film*making*', in turn, is understood here as the active act of exercising all the creative facets of the medium in the process of momentarily gleaning forms out of the elemental forces that make up both images and subjects to be (re)presented.

A crucial point in relation to Deren's, Dulac's and Epstein's propositions about the nature of the medium is that they were presented by filmmakers. That is to say, they were written by people who were not merely reflecting on the medium, but who spent their entire careers exploring what these propositions might mean in practice, developing specific ways of using the camera and editing techniques that may best manifest them. Filmmaker theorists offer particularly perceptive views on the medium as their questions and postulations come from knowing what it is *to film*, rather than from merely encountering film texts as cultural artefacts. My own methodology is deeply informed by the work of these authors: both in the way the project as a whole combines writing and filmmaking, and in the way the book is organised. This is to say, I do not write about *films*, but rather about *film* and *filmmaking*. It is for this reason that the book is not so much concerned with analysing existing work by others but first and foremost with developing modes of filmmaking in response to specific questions and challenges arising from other disciplines, and with using practical filmmaking to generate insights that will be valuable across disciplines. While I hope the book will make a contribution to the broader discourse of environmental humanities and media studies, I also see it in large part as existing in the lineage of the written work of all the above-mentioned filmmaker theorists. It is to this conversation that I want to add: I am writing this book as a filmmaker and in no small part *for* filmmakers.

In what follows I have taken the first steps towards outlining what I came to call 'geological filmmaking', but this concept far surpasses this project or my own filmmaking practice. While the practical challenges encountered in the making of the films helped me flesh out the conceptualisation of geological filmmaking, the term in no way excludes existing or future work of other artists, many of whom engage with similar questions. 'Geological filmmaking' is echoed in the names of some other recent collaborative moving-image projects, such as Geocinema and New Mineral Collective. While their aims and focus differ somewhat from those of my own project – with the 'geo' in Geocinema standing for global communications systems and their image-making capacities, and the New Mineral Collective working through speculative performative methods that centre the body and affect as sites of extraction – we all share an ecology of practices. It is also to this broader ecology of practices that my book is addressed, not only in its combination of theory and practice but also in its sense of openness which positions geological filmmaking as both a concept and a methodology. It is a concept that can be picked up on a way towards a further theorisation of the rich variety of the ongoing film practice that shares similar concerns. And it is a methodology that can be taken up by other artists, hopefully to be developed and transformed in ways that only future will tell.

As for the methodological aspects of geological filmmaking, for me the process begins from a sense of awe in the face of a particular nonhuman entity. In the case of this project such entities were a geological material and a land formation – asbestos and sinkholes – but they need not be *just* geological. In practicing the methodology of geological filmmaking, the filmmaking does not follow the outcomes of researching the films' subject matter to illustrate what had been found out. Instead, new knowledge is produced through the practical challenge of depicting the matter at hand visually. Indeed, in order to use filmmaking to discover something new, it is crucial to remain open to discovering something new about filmmaking. Producing new knowledge through filmmaking does not mean applying a static notion of filmmaking to a new film subject, but rather allowing for filmmaking to be fluid and to push at its boundaries in an effort to grasp the subject. The starting point for geological filmmaking is thus a dual motivation to learn more about the nonhuman entity through film as well as about the medium of film itself. The very first instance of a reciprocity between film and geology lies in this dual openness of the wonder elicited by the subject of the film and of the ongoing curiosity towards the possibilities of the medium of film. Cinematic formal constraints as well as cinematic technologies thus become as worthy of investigation as the subject of the film, and can be as determining of the film's outcome as any intentions of its human author.

There is, however, no getting away from the human author. Alongside the initial encounters with the non-human subject of the film and its technological means, the starting point of the methodology of geological filmmaking also involves accounting for one's own role as author or maker. In the first instance, this entails understanding oneself as a member of the species that exists in a precarious and perhaps unsustainable relationship with its environment. It also involves understanding oneself as a specifically situated human subject, embedded in particular political, geographic and ecological microcosms, which differentially affect and are affected by the subjects of the films as well as the worst of the current symptoms of the ecological crisis. For example, in my case, studying the history of asbestos highlighted the pivotal role that Russia, where I am originally from, has played in asbestos' continued extraction and marketisation long after the revelations of its toxicity. Having grown up in Russia, there is good reason to believe the schools I went to as a child were insulated with asbestos, and to worry whether it was safely contained. With that, I also had to consider myself as a material entity. Grappling with one's own position as author thus also means understanding oneself as a body made from mostly organic matter, constantly cycling environmental matter through its system. In the case of my project, the initial consideration of myself as both a socio-economic subject and a fleshy sponge provided a foundation for what the films later brought into sharp relief: the entangled and reciprocal co-emergence of the socio-economic and the geologic, and of our mortal bodies and environments.

The formal decisions that go into shooting and later editing in the process of geological filmmaking emerge out of the above considerations of all the actors involved in the making of the films: the nonhuman subjects of the films, the moving image medium and the filmmaking equipment, as well as the author as a situated human subject *and* a material body. If such consideration can perhaps be described as an initial *conceptual* encounter with and between these actors, then the process of making the films offers a *material* encounter between them. For example, in the extreme heat of shooting *Salarium* the encounter of the environment with both the equipment and my body meant that almost the entire film was produced in the ninety-second intervals between air-conditioning breaks. The way this material necessity circumscribed the process necessarily informed every individual decision, while the strain on the body as well as the camera inspired every formal experiment. Throughout the making of both films there were constant reminders that there is only so much that is physically possible, but that precisely in touching that boundary there is a lot to learn. The very foundation of *Asbestos* was defined by this fact, as the film pursued the impossible task of dealing with a submicroscopic material through optical means. A key aspect of the methodology of geological filmmaking is that formal choices cannot be premeditated. Rather, they emerge through the real-time unfolding of the encounter between the specificities of all the actors – human, nonhuman and technological – involved in the making of the film at each particular moment. An appreciation of the physical limits of the scope of one's intended actions and a surrender to one's position as an engaged participant in the perpetually unfolding processes, instead of an imposition of one's premeditated plan on them, offer valuable lessons for the broader issues of living in and through the ecological crisis.

Another key aspect of geological filmmaking is that the formal choices that emerge often aim to mimic cinematically the more representationally or perceptually challenging qualities of the subjects of the films. But, importantly, this is not to claim that the resulting films will thus be able to provide some privileged access to their nonhuman subjects or channel them directly. Film, documentary or otherwise, is never a window onto some preexisting reality. The reality that a film creates is always specific *to* film. As Pasi Valiaho puts it, insofar as film is 'a mode of disclosing and bringing forth' the world, 'a way of letting appear and thus generating being', film 'discloses and brings forth the world in a manner specific to itself' (Valiaho 2010, 10). This is not film's limitation – but rather its strength. And, as Deren writes, in shooting and splicing together a film, 'the reality which emerges is a new one' (1946, 39-40). It is arguably film's special privilege that, by exploring and bending its possibilities as a temporal and optical medium, it is capable of creating a new reality. This process takes place as much in shooting as in editing.

In geological filmmaking the approach to editing is not guided by an attempt to replicate the already existent spatial relations or linear causal narratives, but rather by trying to find resonant points of cinematic connection and juxtaposition in the footage and its qualities, and thus create new spatio-temporal arrangements. In this sense, reaching for the elusive nonhuman subjects of the films is really a reaching towards the core of film itself, and there at the core of the formal possibilities and limits of the medium some insights about the films' subjects may be able to come to light. Filmmaking understood as a shaping of spatio-temporal reality can therefore be said to already involve a shaping of the future.

The Geological

While the methodological approach of geological filmmaking outlined above is applicable to ecological relations of every kind, the focus of the case studies that served as prisms for developing this methodology, and for answering the key theoretical questions of the project, are specifically geological. There are a number of reasons for this. One key reason is that moving images, in their materiality, are inherently tied to the material geology of the earth. As technical images they are bound to the earth through their reliance on minerals, metals and chemicals extracted from the ground, often at high environmental cost (Parikka 2015; Cubitt 2017). Their geological materiality ties media, including analogue and digital moving image technologies, to a planetary spatial perspective. Today, some of the most ubiquitous moving image-making tools – smart phones – contain minerals and metals from around the world, from lithium mined in Chile's salt flats to rare earths from Inner Mongolia. As well as being tied to innumerable locations, the temporality of contemporary technical images encompasses the deep past of the formation of the mined materials and fuel required to power and produce the technologies that enable them, as well as the deep future of the material persistence of these technologies. The cinematic intersection with material geology also includes the creation of geological formations on the smaller scale of image capture. Both analogue and digital photographic or cinematic capture happen as a chemical exchange on a molecular level, as photosensitive materials enable a 'chemical conversion of light' (Cubitt 2014, 244). In the case of celluloid film, light oxidises grains of silver halides, while in the case of digital capture, electrons are gathered by the crystal lattice of a CCD sensor. Meanwhile the CCD sensor's crystal lattice itself is fabricated through a process of geological formation: starting from a seed crystal it is grown on the chip, with the molecular structure pre-empting the distribution of the pixels (Cubitt 2014, 105). Moving images, whether analogue or digital, are thus inherently tied to geology on both planetary and molecular scales.

Not merely bound to the earth, every cinematic image is also doubly bound to the sun. An image created by optical capture relies on the presence of light that bounces off objects and onto the photosensitive plane, where it is captured by photochemical substrate or a CCD sensor. This light either comes directly from the sun in the form of sunlight, or it comes from electricity, which for the majority of the history of the film industry came from fossil fuels. The latter has been formed, in turn, by millions of years of sunlight captured in decomposing prehistoric life forms. (Cinematic images generated by processes that bypass optical capture, such as CGI, likewise rely on electricity.) Indeed, the earliest photographic capture process was named *heliography*, or sun writing. Developed by Louis Daguerre's lesser-known collaborator Nicéphore Niépce, the process created an image by capturing light impressed directly upon stone. Niépce created his first photographic images by covering limestone with a layer of bitumen, a naturally occurring petroleum tar, placing an image on it and exposing it to the sun. The bitumen hardened in proportion to its exposure to light, and the less hardened parts could be wiped off with a solvent, leaving a positive image. These experiments led to the invention of what are now known as daguerreotypes, which involved spreading bitumen on a metal sheet placed within a camera obscura: the images were created by a fused stratum of bitumen on the surface of the metal once exposed to the sun. Light is thus a geological force. William Jerome Harrison, a nineteenth-century geologist and photographer, wrote a history of photography that he pitched as 'a natural history rather than a history of signification or representation' (Bobbette

2013, 53). Harrison's history of photography is a geological history (Zylinska 2018), as he saw photographs as much more than representations: he saw them as new geological objects in the world formed in the fusion of bitumen, metal and light. Geological materiality and geological formation therefore underpin the entire history of photochemical image capture, from the birth of photography all the way to contemporary 8K digital cinema.

The second key reason for my focus on the geological in this project of confronting the aesthetic challenges of grasping the relational totality of the ecological crisis is that the geological represents a limit case of the human attempt to grapple with the nonhuman. Through actively engaging with inorganic geological materiality and geological deep time as the furthest removed from the framework of human perception, I hope to create some tools that could be applicable to engaging with other nonhuman aspects of ecologies, aspects that may seem closer to us than the geological but that we nevertheless fail to grasp. The book also seeks to complicate the divisions of life and nonlife, and to show the geological as active. The geological is presented here as deeply intertwined with the organic, the corporeal, the economic and the political, counter to the powers and discourses that had sought to define it as inorganic inert matter, often in service of seeing it as standing reserve.

The geological has been a preoccupation of philosophy since before the establishing of the discipline of geology. As Jeffrey Jerome Cohen puts it, stone is 'philosophy's favorite object' in its metaphorical role as the very embodiment of ontology (2015, 31). In the debate on idealism versus materialism, Samuel Johnson famously refuted George Berkeley's assertion of the material world being '"merely ideal" by forcefully kicking a stone that was not to be moved, declaring "I refute it *thus*"' (Boswell quoted in Cohen 2015, 31). Immanuel Kant, Johann Wolfgang von Goethe and Georg Wilhelm Friedrich Hegel were all actively involved with the emergent discipline of geology. Shocked by the Lisbon earthquake, Kant was involved in the establishment of seismology, Goethe was active in geological debates alongside managing precious metal mines, while Hegel collected minerals and followed the development of palaeontology. Philosophers' fascination with the geological together with its treatment as a given continued into the twentieth century. Jean-Paul Sartre wrote that stone provided an experience of an 'encounter of pure matter', only accessible in divinity and geology (Sartre 1976, 181-182). Jean-Luc Nancy, in turn, used stone as a metaphor for the immovable reality 'at the heart of things' (Nancy 1993, 168).

Such philosophical uses of the geological, however, (mis)understand it as being fixed, that is, as being merely inorganic matter, instead of accounting for the geological's continual flux (even if this flux remains invisible to the human eye). But the geological is not a given. It does not offer 'firm support for ponderous thinking' (Cohen 2015, 31). In the ecological crisis, as the extractivist overreliance on geological materials is leading to the destabilisation of geophysical processes, it is imperative not to think of the geological as a 'self-evident asset [or] inert commodity' (Cohen 2015, 41). Nor is stone worldless, as claimed and dismissed by Martin Heidegger in his enquiry into the relationship between animal and environment (Heidegger 1995). Rather, the geological is intimately intertwined with the organic: minerals are necessary for the functioning of biological bodies and geologic deposits are often made up of organic matter, as is the case with limestone and fossil fuels. It is crucial, then, not only to regard the geological as matter but also to grasp it in its ongoing transformation and relationality.

In the later twentieth century, philosophical uses of the geological as a metaphor moved towards employing the logic of geological processes as a model for the thinking of human history in terms of nonlinear energy flows (De Landa 1997) as well as the stratification and destratification of organised social formations (see Deleuze and Guattari 1987). The contemporary situation of the geophysical crisis, however, calls for a mode of theorising the way in which human history and social formations emerge through the geologic in a material rather than metaphorical sense. As Nigel Clark (2017) suggests, the geological did not just gain political significance in the current crisis. Rather, political formations historically arise in the context of specific geological formations, such as with the stratification of class relations in the context of prospecting for coal and, later, oil. Kathryn Yusoff (2018) further draws a direct relationship between the development of the discipline of geology and the history of colonial racial violence. She positions the discipline of geology as enabling colonialism, by describing geology, with its practices of survey, mapping and classification, as a mode of accumulation and dispossession, and colonialism as an extraction project above all else. Not merely in its direct relationship to the expropriation of natural resources, geology's violent legacy also includes the conceptualisation of the division of life from nonlife: of geology from biology, the organic from the inorganic, active from inert matter, and the human from the inhuman. Yusoff argues that the category of the inhuman, which owes its invention to geology, was responsible for the ability to conceptualise certain humans as inhuman through slavery: the conceptualisation of matter as active or inert was applied to both corporeal and mineralogical matter, rendering an enslaved subject as the nonagentic matter of flesh, or a unit of corporeal energy. The language of geology thus underpinned settler colonialism and slavery in its slippage between the inhuman and the inhumane.

In the current crisis, the enforced division between life and nonlife is responsible not only for *inter*human-nonhuman violence (the destruction of ecosystems), but also for *intra*human violence, where extractivist projects do not just destroy lives and ways of life as a by-product of prioritising the extraction and sale of natural resources, as I will discuss through the industrial history of asbestos in the next chapter, but also actively use the natural environment as one of the tools of colonial occupation, as I will elaborate in relation to sinkholes in chapter three. In order to think of political alternatives to colonial extractive capital, it is crucial to complicate the definitions of the geological and the social all the way down to the separation of the geological from the biological, or life from nonlife. Elizabeth A. Povinelli argues that the division between life and nonlife is demanded and reaffirmed by 'extractive capital and its state allies' (2016, 44), and that the continuation of human and planetary life depends on rethinking how this distinction is postulated. Starting from the definition of life as located in a metabolising organism, she contends that we need merely to shift the scale beyond a single organism to perceive the mutual metabolism of the geological and the biological. This metabolism is the planetary carbon cycle that sees life interact with nonlife through respiration, digestion and death. In death, life sediments in the geological layer as fossil fuels, which, in turn, are seen by extractive capitalism as nonlife, resources to be extracted and burnt into the atmosphere, only to further participate in biological and chemical processes such as ocean acidification. The division of life from nonlife, the organic from the inorganic, active matter from inert matter, does not hold under scrutiny, and thus requires ongoing violent fortification to the benefit of extractivist and imperialist projects – and to the peril of humans and nonhumans alike. By way of an epistemological shift away from this way of thinking, the object of study in my work, and in the specific case studies of asbestos and sinkholes, is not the geologic material or formation *as such*: the object of study is *the very intersection* of the geologic with the embodied and the political.

Geological Time and Film Time

The formation of geological materials and the global processes of erosion and sedimentation that slowly shape the current lines of the landscape take place over millions and billions of years. Geological time is most frequently thought of as deep time: unfathomably vast durations that far outstrip not merely human lifespans but the entire history of the human species. But perhaps equally as unfathomable, and infinitely more urgent to come to grips with, is the temporality of the human intersections with the geological here and now. The temporality of the ecological crisis more broadly, as well as of the attempts to mitigate it, unfolds on a spectrum of often incommensurate scales and contradictory directions. As Maria Puig de la Bellacasa describes in her work on care time, the future 'appears to be pulled forward by an accelerated timeline toward a gloomy environmental future, while the time left for action in the present is compressed by urgency' (2017, 173). At the same time this condition of emergency is at odds with the slowness required in ecological care. Perhaps the most stark and destructive contrast in the temporal scale of the ecological crisis is between the slowness of environmental time and the pace of parliamentary politics. In his thesis on environmental slow violence, Rob

Nixon outlines how 'casualties from slow violence are' out of sync 'with the swift seasons of electoral change', as 'preventative or remedial environmental legislation ... cannot deliver dependable electoral cycle results, even though those results may ultimately be life saving' (2011, 9). While the incommensurability of temporal scales of ecological shifts and parliamentary terms results in the political dismissal of the future, capitalism incorporates and sells the future for present profits. This is particularly stark in futures markets, where the abstraction of the future value of geological resources, from oil to gold, has significant bearing on material realities, both present and future.

Yet, as Yusoff proposes, durability in the crisis depends on the future being non-predetermined, non-singular, non-unilinear and emergent through a complex multiplicity of interacting and interdependent temporalities. She writes that despite our best efforts to secure a future in the changing environment, the future is unpredictable. No activist efforts or legal victories that are localisable can guarantee longevity as there is 'no one decision that is made once and for all' (Yusoff 2013, 213), and today's victories are vulnerable to being undone. Extending our responsibility towards the future thus also means contemplating a time in which we can no longer make a difference. Yusoff argues that in order to conceive of an ethics and politics that goes beyond ourselves temporally, we must begin with thinking beyond localisable objects of our concern in the now. That is to say that in order to devise an ethics that can persist in the time in which we are not, we need to first conceive of an ethics that can hold multiplicity in the present. What Yusoff calls 'ethical duration' is 'not to be conceived as one duration, ... but rather as modalities of duration for the more than one, which have differing durations' (211). In other words, durability within the crisis hinges on our ability to take 'a diversity of timescales into account' (Puig de la Bellacasa 2017, 191-2). Film, a temporal medium at its core, presents a plane on which to engage with a diverse ecology of durations. The temporality of film is also itself full of contradictions and incommensurabilities that coexist. Simultaneously vast and minute, continuous and discontinuous, technological and physiological, the multifaceted temporality of film carries the potential to account for a multiplicity of ecological and geological temporalities.

The question of coexisting and contradictory timeframes has been at the core of cinematic time from its very beginning. Cinema emerged at the end of the nineteenth century into a cultural landscape that saw not only the earth but also time itself being reimagined as a resource by colonial and industrial projects, as the latter became increasingly uniform, homogenised, standardised and rationalised. As Mary Ann Doane explains, the emergence of cinematic time took place amid a 'cultural imperative' for 'the structuring of time and contingency' (2002, 3). Alongside the discoveries around the irreversibility of time through the Second Law of Thermodynamics, and the establishment of universalised world clock time, much of time's standardisation was linked to its becoming, after Marx, a measure of value. For the capitalist to buy a quantity of the labourer's time, time had to be measurable and therefore divisible, which clashed with the longstanding philosophical understanding of time, conceptualised by Henri Bergson during the same historical period as 'uninterrupted transition, multiplicity without divisibility and succession without separation' (Bergson 2002, 205). This dilemma around the (dis)continuous nature of time became the locus of the theoretical discussion surrounding the possibility of its representability. It was then that film emerged and appeared to embody this dilemma: on the one hand it was made up of individual frames, the dreaded instants of time, on the other it was seen as being able to emulate the perception of continuous time. Gilles Deleuze later used the geological metaphor of a crystal to theorise further the ability of the cinematic image to make the dual nature of time in Bergsonian philosophy visible: the split of 'the present into two heterogeneous directions' of the present that passes on and the past that is preserved (Deleuze 2005, 79). With televisual transmission and recording on magnetic tape or via the CCD sensor, the ability of the moving image to create the illusion of continuous motion was no longer tied to separable frames, yet its ability to carry a multiplicity of coexisting temporalities was not diminished.

Cinematic duration can be understood across a variety of scales – from a single frame to deep time, and a variety of perspectives – from a material to a perceptual one. The smallest unit of cinematic duration that perhaps first comes to mind is the time between the frames, which, by definition and by design, occurs beyond the limits of perception. The very possibility of the illusion of motion created by cinema requires this time interval to effectively disappear. Early cinema emerged hand in hand with the physiological experiments into the precise interval that was needed for image retention to be achieved. As Holl argues, 'looking to the prehistory of cinema in the psycho-physiological laboratories we can see that models developed in the laboratory of how the mind and the psychology of the senses works exactly corresponded to the structure of cinematic perception' (2017, 35). She elaborates that the first cinematic apparatuses relied on the research in image retention and the perception of motion, pointing to an alliance between 'the functions of the apparatuses … with the functions of the nervous system' (42). The first unit of cinematic duration is thus determined by the human neurological system. In the silent era this interval fluctuated between sixteen and twenty-four frames per second, but with the introduction of sound this number had to be standardised, and what was settled on was twenty-four.

With the introduction of digital moving image, new technological possibilities arose for both the capture and display of cinematic images, and the notion of a cohesive gap between frames disappeared. As Cubitt writes, 'whereas analog cinema dissects time into discrete but whole moments, through the clock function and scanning, digital images ensure that there is never a whole, complete, coherent image' (2014, 251). Each frame appears one pixel at a time and has a duration of its own. Thus in digital moving image 'the frame itself is a temporal phenomenon' (251), becoming the smallest measure of cinematic duration. By doing away with the discreet succession of analogue frames, the smallest measure of cinematic duration is in fact defined by constant, continuous and imperceptible change.

The duration of a film frame can be reconsidered further from the perspective of the material factors involved in exposing it: hardware and light. If exposed by sunlight, the duration of each frame can be thought to contain the eight minutes and twenty seconds that it takes light to travel from the sun to the earth. If exposed by artificial lighting, in turn, the frame can be thought to contain the temporality of the electricity that powered the light, be it derived from fossil fuels, nuclear fission, water, wind or sun. Behind the registration of every film frame there is also the material history of the hardware that makes the image capture possible: the deep time of the formation of the materials from which the camera is made. Thus in every film frame the duration of the minutely imperceptible process of the registration of light upon celluloid or a CCD sensor becomes commensurate with the vastly imperceptible millions of years it took for the formation of fossil fuels, metals and minerals to occur.

Further contemplating the temporality of even a single film frame from a media archaeological perspective, its duration also includes the duration of media history's sedimentation. As Parikka puts is, 'the media-technological artifact as a monument is a reminder from a past media culture, and as such carries with itself pastness', with each machine itself being 'a concrete form of the principles, diagrams, examples of past media in action' (2012, 132). Media history is seen here not as a teleological progression of 'one-thing-after-another', but as being akin to geological time, where each formation carries the trace of its emergence. The duration of a film frame thus also includes the duration of the history of all proto-cinematic technologies.

Expanding outwards from the frame, cinematic duration includes the duration of each individual shot of the film, the duration of the film as a whole and the future of the film. The duration of the film itself has a multiplicity of dimensions that include the material (for example, the physical length of the film reel, which exists independently of being screened or seen) and the perceptual (the length of the cinematic experience when the film is screened), the perceptual dimension of course itself having a material dimension that spans the hardware on which the film is played to the audience members' eyes and ears. From the perceptual perspective, the future of the cinematic experience expands into the time in which the film 'reverberates across the space between the film world and the real world, seeping into conversations and dreams, tinting the world and making it vibrate in particular ways, injecting thought-images, sensations, motivations, heightened attunements to one thing or another, into the larger social and ecological fields within which the film's signs, meanings, and affects resound' (Ivakhiv 2013, 12-13). From the material perspective, the temporality of a given film expands into the future: in the medium term into a media paradigm where the film text disappears as the celluloid rots or the digital file becomes corrupted or unreadable, and upon a geologic scale into the deep future of media technological fossils (Parikka 2015), where the fossilised remains of film technologies far outstrip the lives of the film's viewers, creators or the civilisation to which cinema owes its invention.

From a single frame and beyond, cinematic duration is capable of containing a multiplicity of temporal scales, which are determined relationally by the physiological capabilities of the human eye to see motion and the capabilities of the cinematic apparatus to register light, all the way to the future deep time in which the minerals, metals and chemicals that make up the cinematic hardware will decompose. The material and temporal intersections of film and the geological discussed above apply to every cinematic image. This is the material and theoretical foundation upon which the further part of my project builds. Given that this state of events can be taken as a given with all filmmaking, my own project takes it upon itself to develop a mode of filmmaking directly in response to this fact. With all of the above in mind, the following two chapters take on this task through the prism of two specific geological case studies focused on asbestos and sinkholes, and through approaching two key aesthetic challenges presented by the ecological crisis, one surrounding perception, the other – depiction.

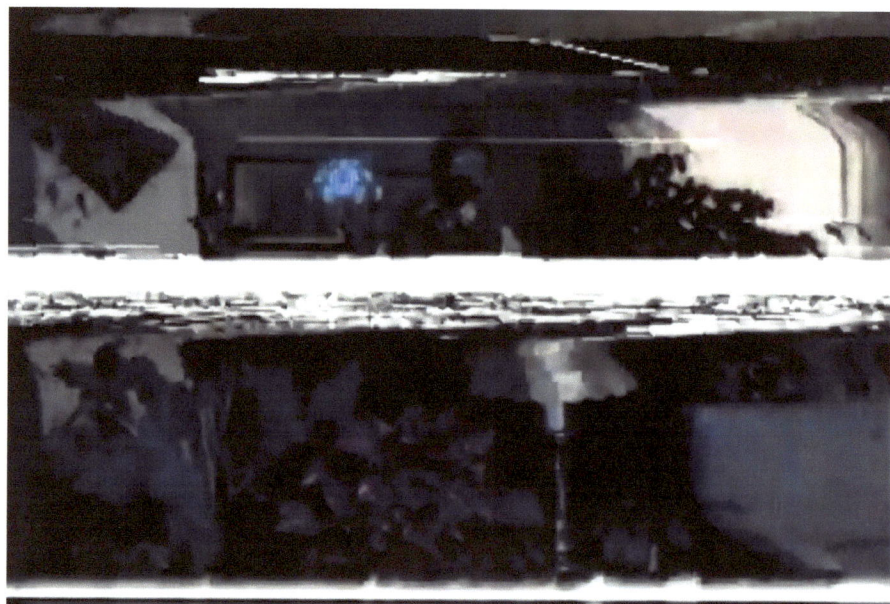

Fig 2. Still from *Asbestos* (2016), Sasha Litvintseva and Graeme Arnfield.

CHAPTER 2

Perception: Asbestos

Shot on magnetic tape and perhaps stored incorrectly, the image has clearly been corroded by time. The tape has disintegrated in the intervening decades and the footage it carries has become corrupted. This is most immediately evident in the colour of the image: the tape has lost its ability to reproduce natural colour and appears on a grey-blue scale, with flesh showing as blue, plants as purple and much else in greyscale. The scene is an interior wide shot, with a presenter positioned in the middle of the frame somewhat to the back of the room, surrounded with plants and lamps to the sides and in the foreground. 'How do you know if you have an asbestos problem in your building? What does an asbestos problem look like?' he ponders. 'Well, that's a big part of the problem, because with asbestos the problem is invisible'. As soon as he says the word 'invisible', an intense static distortion starts travelling across the screen in jagged black and white lines, obscuring the image. The static continues as he continues speaking: 'the kinds of fibres that are most dangerous to the human body and are most prone to be airborne' and here the sound cuts out for a few moments to come back on, '... the human eye'. The part of the phrase that gets erased in the midst of the damage to the tape is 'invisible to (the human eye)'.

The clip is from a 1980s amateur documentary on the molecular structure, potential health hazards, detection and removal of asbestos. It also appears in my film *Asbestos* (2016), made in parallel with this chapter and discussed in it. Both of these films in their different ways try to grapple with the most insidious aspect of the toxic material: its invisibility. Invisibility, of course, presents quite a challenge to an optical visual medium. It is also one of the key aesthetic challenges posed by the ecological crisis, which encapsulates numerous processes that are either invisible or that defy human perceptual experience due to their dispersed spatial and temporal scale. These range from the deep time of the half-life of radioactive materials and the invisibility of radiation, to the estimated extinction of species never previously sighted. The key question guiding this chapter is how it might be possible to visually engage with an invisible aspect of the environmental crisis and what such an attempt would make intelligible instead.

What is so remarkable about this distorted clip is the way the *intentional* verbal content of the narration *about* invisibility interacts with the *unintentional* material disintegration that *causes* the invisibility of the image and the inaudibility of the soundtrack. But the invisibility or inaudibility of the content that was intentionally created by the filmmakers is not merely a lack or absence; rather, it is an active perceptible presence. What we see in the static and what we hear in the silence, which swallows the moment where the words 'invisible to' would have been, are the materiality and temporality of the media artefact. The disintegration of the tape has given form to the imperceptible itself, revealing it to be implacable material agencies operating alongside human intentionality and unfolding in time. Over the course of this chapter I will continue to explore the interaction of human and nonhuman agencies at the core of the question of invisibility through the prism of asbestos and the film I made about it. But, first, it is important for me to establish the relational nature of (in)visibility as such.

On the Relationality of (In)Visibility

The limits of the visible world are delineated by perceptual apparatuses, be they biological or technological. As such, they are bound up with the history of scientific visualisation and optical technologies, and with the relationship between instruments, witnessing and knowing. As Joseph Vogl shows in his essay on Galileo and the telescope, the visibilities produced by the newly invented instruments don't bring us closer to being able to see the world exhaustively but rather make us aware of the newly invisible, engendering an infinity of further invisibilities. By making some things that were previously invisible, such as distant stars, visible, the telescope introduced 'an alterable horizon of the visible' (Vogl 2007, 21), where better telescopes could provide access to more distant stars yet. Every form of visibility thus bears 'a stigma of provisionality', surrounded as it is 'by an ocean of invisibility' (22). Such an awareness of the growing wealth of the as-yet invisible shows that 'with every deepening of clarity comes a new depth of the unclarifiable' (22). Every attempt to produce knowledge about the world through making things visible produces knowledge about what is as yet unknowable. More numerous and better technologies do not therefore mean a better, and progressively more exhaustive, understanding of the world – or of our place within it. Technological advances push back the limits of visibility while producing constituent invisibility. Vogl also situates the first instance of the denaturing of vision in the telescope. He argues that 'the telescope does not enlarge any more than the eye makes smaller, and the telescopic view is no less natural than the eye's vision is artificial' (17), demonstrating with this that the telescope and the eye are but two in a sea of infinite potential optical systems and perceptual positions. It is thus with extending the capabilities of the natural eye that the limits of its capabilities are revealed.

During the nineteenth century scientific representations and visualisations were also undergoing a revolution, as the quest for scientific objectivity underwent a shift towards the photographic. As Lorraine Daston and Peter Galison elaborate in their study of objectivity, 'as oracles speaking nature's own language, the inscription instruments ... could actually *become* the ideal observers science had always sought' (1992, 116). In a quest for objectivity that was as moral as it was scientific, photographs promised to succeed where the 'all-too-human scientist' failed: to 'restrain themselves from imposing their hopes, expectations, generalizations, aesthetics, even ordinary language on the image of nature' (81). However, photographs, 'burdened with detail not found in the reader's own specimens, produced in black and white, often blurred to boot', frequently faltered when it came to accuracy (117). The objectivity they were thought to have provided was rooted not in precision and resemblance but in automation and authenticity: the elimination of the human hand. Yet, as Donna Haraway contends, neither the human nor the machine gaze is ever fully neutral or objective, as vision is always a question of power. In her 'Situated Knowledges' essay, Haraway puts forward the idea that any thinking around vision has to account for one's position as the one 'doing' the seeing, be it with or without the aid of technical apparatuses. She argues against 'the god trick of seeing everything from nowhere' (1988, 581), i.e. the objectifying and supposedly distant and neutral gaze that claims 'the power to see and not be seen, to represent while escaping representation' (581). As a way to defy the 'violence implicit in our visualizing practices' (585), Haraway puts forth situated objectivity and partial perspective. She points to the necessarily perspectival position of any view, and the necessary biotechnological apparatus that embodies and mediates it.

In outlining her onto-epistemology Karen Barad writes that 'one must inquire into the material specificities of the apparatuses that help constitute objects and subjects' (2007, 27). She draws on Niels Bohr's experiments on the wave/particle behaviour of electrons, where the electrons consistently exhibited one type of behaviour – either that of a wave or a particle – with the use of one experimental apparatus, and another type of behaviour with the use of a different one. The ability of the apparatus to influence the nature of the observed phenomena challenges the ontology of classical physics and the epistemological assumption 'that experiments reveal the preexisting determinate nature of the entity being measured' (106), showing instead that 'observation-independent objects ... do not preexist as such' (114). 'Apparatuses are not passive observing instruments' (142), and the world that is available to knowledge is only the world in which we had intervened. When it comes to seeing at molecular or atomic scales, using transmission electron or scanning tunnelling microscopes respectively, Barad suggests that 'seeing' becomes a physical intervention in itself. Such microscopes do not merely zoom in further than optical microscopes but operate according to an entirely different set of physical principles that redefine what can be considered as vision. I will return to this point further in the chapter, as it was the invention of the transmission electron microscope that was the turning point in the industrial history of asbestos.

The view created by the eye, the telescope or the transmission electron microscope 'implies its own construction', for in all cases the object seen, be it a landscape, a previously unseen distant star or the molecular structure of asbestos, 'implies the technical operation that makes it visible' (Vogl 2007, 18). Or, as Haraway puts it, 'the "eyes" made available in modern technological sciences shatter any idea of passive vision; these prosthetic devices show us that all eyes, including our own organic ones, are active perceptual systems, building on translations and specific ways of seeing, that is, ways of life' (Haraway 1988: 583). Optical and visualising technologies are not merely sense-prostheses for human vision, they are 'not just an extension of the senses nor an auxiliary device to improve or correct the senses' (Vogl 2007: 17), but devices with their own agencies and positions that expand the very definitions of the sense of sight. The cinematic apparatus is one such technology.

The cinematic image is constituted not only by the impression of the light reflected off objects positioned in front of the camera, but also by all the material forces affecting the recording surface during and after the shoot. In this way film has the capacity to reach things that are invisible to the human eye, potentially including imperceptible aspects of the ecological crisis. One of these is nuclear radiation. In fact, photosensitive substrate's sensitivity to nuclear radiation is responsible for the very discovery of radioactivity: in 1886 the physicist Henri Becquerel serendipitously placed uranium salts on a photographic plate in a dark drawer, later finding the plate fogged, thus evidencing radioactive exposure. One of the most famous pieces of irradiated footage was a roll of film shot by a film crew that flew over Chernobyl three days after the catastrophe in order to document the fallout, physical damage and decontamination efforts following the explosion and meltdown of the nuclear reactor. After the footage was processed and screened, it appeared to be distorted: a snowfall of sparkling incandescent markings plagued the surface of the image. Thinking at first that the film stock was defective from the start, the filmmaker Vladimir Shevchenko realised that 'what he had captured on film was the image and sound of radioactivity itself, as decaying particles moved through the exterior casing of the movie camera to remolecularise his film' (Schuppli 2011, 28-29). The substrate of the film was transformed beyond human intentionality. More than the documentary images of the destroyed power plant that the film crew had set out to capture, these abstract traces evidenced the presence of radiation during their creation. Susan Schuppli uses this event as an example in introducing her new operative concept of 'material witnesses': 'nonhuman entities and machinic ecologies that archive their complex interactions with the world, producing ontological transformations and informatic dispositions that can be forensically decoded and reassembled back into a history' (2020, 3). In this framework, images are able to testify not through the content of what is recorded but through the visible impact to their material support, a support which has been damaged by the violent historical forces or events to which those images thus bear witness.

The Chernobyl film bears material witness to the presence of radiation; it is created by physical impact with radiation and, as such, reveals radiation to be neither invisible nor immaterial. It features 'images' made *by* radiation rather than *of* it, having been impressed directly into the celluloid by the material impact rather than by exposure to light reflected off objects. Light is of course itself a kind of radiation: a solar radiation. The difference between nuclear radiation and light is one of degree, not kind. Gamma rays, the most dangerous and penetrating of ionising rays that together form nuclear radiation, are part of the same electromagnetic spectrum as visible light. At one end of the spectrum, with the lowest frequency, longest wave and least energy, are radio waves, microwaves and infrared waves. The colour red is the first to appear in the visible spectrum, its waves being shorter and its frequency higher than those of infrared waves. The difference in frequency between all the visible colours is minuscule as compared to the entire spectrum, and yet those differences account for the entirety of our experience of the visible world. As the frequency and energy rise and the waves shorten, visible violet gives way to ultraviolet, then to x-ray radiation, and, finally, with the highest energy and frequency of any wave in the spectrum, to gamma rays.

The question of radiation's (in)visibility is not a question of a set external physical property, but rather of the relationship between the abilities of perceptual apparatuses, biological and technological ones, and the properties of the object or wave in question. Jean-François Lyotard addresses the discrepancies between the physical properties of matter and the human perceptual apparatus in *The Inhuman* (1991). Drawing on Bergson, he uses the example of the colour red to show that the reason we perceive it as a static property of an object rather than a vibration is due to the discrepancy in speed between its frequency, 400 trillion vibrations per second, and the time the human eye needs 'to make a temporal dissociation between two pieces of information', two thousandths of a second (Lyotard 1991, 42). If the eye were somehow able to synchronise 'itself to that rhythm, it would no longer perceive red at all' (42), but rather the individual waves, 'instant by instant, each of those shocks itself' (43). Our eyes, optic nerves, and brains' processing power constitute the visible world as much as the physical properties of the observable phenomena. In other words, the visible world is constituted by the relationship between what there is to see and the means by which the seeing is done.

We cannot see the gamma rays with our naked eye or with optical apparatuses, but they can 'see' us. As Timothy Morton quips about gamma rays and x-rays: 'they see you. They see you so intensely that in sufficient quantities they kill you' (2016, 170). Visibility here is not only relational – it is reciprocal. Gamma rays are a product of the radioactive decay of atomic nuclei and are highly penetrating. They are unreachable by optics, but are able to penetrate through walls, protective clothing and biological matter while ionising particles in it, which can lead to cancer and the mutation or even death of cells. Visible light, by contrast, is not able to penetrate the body, apart from the lens of the eye: visible light bounces off the external boundaries of objects, rather than penetrating their insides. It is this quality of visible light that has historically painted vision as a form of perception that does not intervene, that is able to happen at a distance, and that is able to be one-sided and objective – a set of positions that has been challenged by Haraway, Barad and Vogl. Analogue celluloid substrate, though designed to replicate the world as seen by the human eye, is receptive to the entire upper range of the electromagnetic spectrum, from visible light to ultraviolet, x-ray (as evidenced by the advice to not let undeveloped film go through the x-ray machines at the airport) and high-energy particles, or gamma rays. The irradiated footage is thus also a reminder of the fact that cinematic and photographic images are, as characterised by Cubitt, 'interventions in the physical processes of the world' that are 'evidence only of a photon, not of the existence of whatever surface it bounced off last' (2014, 246). A photosensitive surface, be it analogue or digital, produces 'a record of light, not things' (244). Whether created by solar or nuclear radiation, this record is a nonhuman witness to a chemical reaction, over and above its anthropogenic mobilisation toward figuration.

As we have seen, nuclear radiation is separated from visible light merely by an order of degree rather than kind and is able to not only make itself visible but also to create images by impacting the film surface on a subatomic level. Most other imperceptible aspects of the ecological crisis, however, are neither a current that can impact the film surface directly nor a contained object that can reflect light, and are thus both materially and optically unavailable to the film image. In order to explore the question driving this part of the project, my goal has been to identify a subject that would encompass being unavailable to the naked eye or to optical microscopes as well as being the result of the fallout of industrial activity, being dispersed around the world and persistent over vast geological timescales. But, given that thinking the geological and the perceptual together, as is the aim of this research project and this specific chapter, necessarily involves thinking the geological alongside the embodied, I have also been interested in finding an imperceptible nonhuman agent that, like radiation, is able to enter and alter organic bodies, thus highlighting 'the intimacy, porosity, and permeability of humans and human organizations within the web of life' (Moore 2015, 7).

The mineral asbestos encompasses all of these qualities. Once broadly used in industrial and architectural applications due to its inflammable and durable qualities, submicroscopic airborne asbestos was found to be fatally toxic when inhaled. The history of its use and disuse is tied up with the history of the advance of scientific visualising technologies, as the turning point in its industrial history hinged on the invention of non-optical microscopes, prior to which airborne asbestos was undetectable. Approaching asbestos cinematically, and specifically through a practical investigation, becomes a challenge when it comes to the possibility of imaging an invisible and latent atmospheric threat – a challenge that is emblematic of the visual culture of the ecological crisis. Asbestos, its promise and its downfall also present a prism through which to study the non-linear, complex and contradictory industrial history of the past century. In what follows I develop the argument around the relational nature of visibility and the reciprocal nature of perception. By examining the haptic qualities of both the toxicity and visibility of asbestos, I present perception as permeability: I look at perception from the outside and the inside, and at the journey between the two.

Asbestos: Toxic and Haptic

Asbestos is thought to have been discovered and used in Ancient Greece over four thousand years ago, with the earliest uses including cremation cloths and perpetual lamp wicks. The name itself originates with the Roman natural philosopher Pliny the Elder, and his use of *asbestinon*, Latin for 'unquenchable'. In his *Natural History*, Pliny mistakenly identifies the provenance of the material as growing 'in the deserts of India, scorched by the burning rays of the sun' and therefore as being 'habituated to resist the action of fire' (Pliny the Elder 1855, book 19, chap. 4). Despite the fallaciousness of this origin myth, the industrial use of asbestos, which expanded dramatically in the first half of the twentieth century, reflected precisely this quality. The applications of asbestos ranged from filters in early gas masks and fireproof fireman suits to its more broadly known uses as a heat and electric insulator, in brake linings and in construction and as a fire-retardant in roofing, walls and floors. Some early-envisaged uses were more eccentric than this. For example, in a letter published in the *New York Times* in 1866, an entrepreneur writes: asbestos is as 'pliant as any silk' and due to its 'incombustible nature' it would be able to 'set aside the vexatious expense and use of soap and water, for all a lady will have to do when she unrobes herself, will be to pitch her articles of apparel into a glowing fire, and when they have become as white as a snowflake she may resume them at her pleasure' (Anonymous 1866, 5). This application of asbestos never caught on, but in the space of merely a decade asbestos extraction on an industrial scale was already underway. Writing in 1888, Robert H. Jones called it 'one of Nature's most marvellous productions' (1888, 5), while a 1909 *New York Times* article suggested that 'of all the queer materials which nature seems to have provided for no other purpose than that man may show his ingenuity in their use, nothing compares to that mineralogical vegetable, asbestos' (Anonymous 1909, 6). Such flamboyant excitement feels chillingly foreboding with the benefit of hindsight.

Asbestos is not a specific mineral but rather an umbrella term for a group of silicate minerals with a fibrous structure: chrysotile, amosite and crocidolite being the most frequently mined and used varieties. Although the formulae for the asbestos minerals show them to contain a number of ubiquitous elements, it is their physical attributes on a molecular level that dictate both their industrial usage and their health hazards. The advances in imaging technology have revealed that asbestos is 'formed through polymerization, the repetition of a chemical unit in a linear array' (Skinner, Rossa and Frondel 1988, 11). This means that 'a fiber visible to the naked eye is formed by the aggregation of thousands of elongate submicroscopic linear arrays' (11) and can be pulverised indefinitely, breaking down into ever smaller forms, until we are left with a chain that is one molecule thick. As such, it is invisible not only to the naked eye but also to optical microscopes. The industrial usages of asbestos were indebted to precisely this fibrous nature of the mineral as it allowed the material to be highly flexible, durable and, crucially, capable of being woven into and through any other industrial material, from roofing to wall insulation. In other words, the industrial uses of asbestos drew on its ability to be highly malleable and capable of being materially entangled with other materials, of losing itself in them by making them infused with itself.

The toxicity of asbestos arises out of the very same physical properties: it is the fibrous nature of its molecular structure that allows for its entanglement with organic tissue. The submicroscopic shards of asbestos are a shape and size that enable them to become airborne and, when they come into contact with a human cell, to physically pierce it like a needle. In contrast with nuclear radiation – an immaterial ray that impacts organic matter on a subatomic level by ionising particles in it, which changes their charge by making them lose or acquire electrons – airborne asbestos is made up of physical particles whose encounter with organic matter is that of a direct physical impact. Though only one molecule thick, and indeed precisely because they are only one molecule thick, shards of asbestos are able to penetrate cells to become foreign bodies in the biological environment. This initiates 'cellular responses to an unexpected trauma, and a normal repair mechanism [is] the deposition of a fibrous protein, collagen, in excessive concentrations at the site of trauma', which can result in mesothelioma, a cancer of the lining of the lungs from asbestos inhalation, which usually arises out of asbestos exposure that 'may have been relatively mild and taken place over 30 years before' (Skinner 2003, 3). More immediate and more common among those that mined and processed the material, asbestosis is an often fatal fibrosis of the lungs, caused by excessive forming of scar tissue 'to encapsulate the non-normal additions to the normally soft tissue environment' (3), which in sufficient quantities deform the lining of the lungs and constrict breathing. When asbestos enters the lungs, it triggers a reaction and is absorbed as the tissue is transformed, forming an aggregate that is only possible in their connection.

The history of asbestos-related illnesses is as long as the history of its use, with suspicions around it being a cause of illness in those that worked with it dating back to the first century A.D. Dangers of asbestos exposure, and therefore associated health complications, are unevenly distributed, with workers at asbestos mines, refineries and now abatement and removal industries being most at risk. The history of asbestos is thus also a history of international class struggle in industrial capitalism. The first cases of asbestos-related deaths in asbestos-processing factories were documented in the nineteenth century. In the 1920s the increasing number of fatalities among the workers at the Rochdale asbestos processing plant near Manchester led to first official diagnoses of asbestosis. And yet asbestos extraction and use continued to grow until the mid-twentieth century.

It was not until 1972 that restrictions on the amount of airborne asbestos allowed in the workplace began to be put in place, becoming progressively stricter over the following decades, before asbestos was officially banned in EU member states in 1999. Though these official restrictions followed the revelations of asbestos's molecular structure, and therefore scientific proof of its toxicity, they also followed decades of legal and activist struggle. These are struggles that continue to this day, for the history of the use and disuse of asbestos is also geographically uneven, as 'advances in occupational health in certain parts of the world have gone hand-in-hand with testimonies to the alleged safety of working with asbestos in other parts of the world' (Gregson, Watkins and Calestani 2010, 1066). As Europe and North America moved to ban asbestos, the Global

South became progressively more exposed. As Kathryn Yusoff writes in her analysis of the 'racialized relations of power' of geology, exposure to its toxic legacy is resolutely cut 'along color lines' (2018, 10). This has been manifestly true in the export markets of asbestos over the recent decades. Canada, once the producer of forty percent of the world's asbestos, only stopped extraction in 2012, having exported it for decades, in large part to India, despite the ban on its domestic use. I will further elaborate on the Canadian context of asbestos industries in the following part of the chapter.

The invisibility of asbestos, or rather its visual elusiveness when it comes to the naked eye and optical microscopes, has played a key role in the history of its use and disuse. The placement and subsequent enforcement of restrictions on airborne asbestos would not have been possible without the invention of the transmission electron microscope, which allowed for its detection. It was also thanks to the progress in imaging technologies, from the transmission electron microscope and spectroscopy to electron diffraction, that the physical properties of both asbestos molecules and human cells, as well as the relationship between the two, could be understood better. While optical microscopes use glass lenses to focus light upon the object of study, which then reflects back, transmission electron microscopes use electromagnetic lenses to focus a beam of electrons that travels *through* the object of study, sensing its structure on a molecular level. As Barad contends, a transmission electron microscope 'works on a different set of physical principles than optical microscopes, it undermines any illusion that the image represents the mere magnification of what we see with our eyes' (Barad 2007, 51). As the image created through electron microscopy is achieved through physical contact between the object and tool of observation, Barad suggests that it can be 'more aptly likened to an encounter that engages the sense of touch rather than sight' (52). Transmission electron microscopes have challenged the conception of vision as an immaterial perceptual sense that remains on the outside of the objects of observation: on the molecular level visibility is haptic.

Just as asbestos itself materially traverses the boundaries of inside and outside, the technology that makes it visible penetrates through the object of observation, rather than observing it from the outside. Both the toxicity and visibility of asbestos are manifest in the physical contact of two material entities: the fibre and the cell in the case of toxicity, and the fibre and the beam of electrons that passes through it in the case of visibility. Ordinarily the event of touch occurs on the surface of the body, when an outer boundary of one body comes into contact with an outer boundary of another body. Asbestos, however, is able to breach the boundaries of bodies and interfere with them on a cellular level, destabilising the integrity of what appears to be singular and bounded. The visibility and toxicity of asbestos are thus manifested through touch and, in both cases, they demand a relation of hapticity that goes beyond the idea of surface.

Asbestos: Inside and Outside

The first stages of the methodology of geological filmmaking involve the consideration of the nonhuman subject of the film, the film medium and the human author – and the staging of an initial conceptual encounter between them. In the above account of the history and materiality of asbestos it has been established that both the toxicity and visibility of asbestos are defined by material entanglement and the breaching of the boundaries between inside and outside. Herein lies one potential approach for a filmic engagement with asbestos: it can be seen not as an attempt to make that which is unavailable to optics visible, but as an attempt to follow the traces of its material entanglements and to traverse the boundaries asbestos has traversed.

Film is an optical medium and therefore the biggest practical filmmaking challenge in approaching asbestos is how to capture an object of inquiry that specifically evades optical apparatuses. In the making of any film it is necessary to make a succession of decisions: what to shoot, how to shoot it (how to frame each image, how the camera should or should not move), how to structure the material in the edit (what the overall arc is, what the micro and macro rhythms are, how any two images meet, what the relationship between image and sound is). It is not necessary to be making these decisions creatively or even consciously: *making* a film is by definition the process of making these decisions. Making these decisions *consciously* is where the creativity of filmmaking lies. In geological filmmaking all of these decisions are made directly in relation to the non-human subject of the film.

Asbestos presents an impasse directly in relation to the first question: what to film? Given that it itself is unavailable to the reach of the film lens, the focus has to shift away from the invisible material and towards the possibility of depicting its effects, its production and its material legacy: asbestos has to be depicted in its relationality. Where to look for asbestos's material legacy in the present? Following the visibility-driven revelations of asbestos's toxicity, the asbestos industry has far from ceased. Some of it has merely relocated out of the developed countries, and much of it has shape-shifted into an asbestos removal industry, where extraction from the earth has been replaced with equally industrialised extraction from the walls. Cinematically tracing the logics of these two kinds of extraction – extraction from the earth and extraction from the walls, and the impact they have had and continue to have on bodies and spaces – can provide an entry point to the first question of *what* to film, as well as the formal questions of *how*.

I am not the sole author in the production of both films that are part of this research project. Rather, human agency is collaboratively distributed to offer a multiplicity of perspectives. The film *Asbestos* (2016) involved the coming together of two very different filmmaking approaches. It was made collaboratively with my friend and found-footage filmmaker Graeme Arnfield. Our shared aim was to do justice to the multiple dimensions and contradictions inherent to the material. When beginning the process, we did not know that we would divide the task of procuring the images; rather it was through deeper engagement with the material and its history that this emerged as the desired approach for the subject matter. Every aspect of asbestos seemed to come with a flipside: lifesaving as a fire-retardant yet lethally toxic when inhaled, a solid and visible mineral when extracted from the earth and invisible and toxic when airborne, mined from the earth for industrial use and mined from walls and roofs to counteract its prior application, found to be toxic and banned in the West decades ago yet still in use elsewhere in the world. We wanted the film to be able to allow the contradictions that define asbestos to coexist side-by-side without being resolved. We ultimately found that the most appropriate and, paradoxically, the most collaborative way to approach this aspect would be to divide the tasks of creating and collecting the images and then edit the film together. I would travel to and document a site crucial to the extraction history of asbestos, while Arnfield would collect the found footage of the arduous and ongoing labour of asbestos removal, from around the world and across decades.

As Stacy Alaimo writes, 'matters of environmental concern and wonder are always "here", as well as "there", simultaneously local and global' (2010, 15). In the case of asbestos, large-scale mining only took place in a handful of locations, including Canada, Russia and South Africa, and the material was then distributed all around the world. As the location for the site to which I would travel to shoot the ever-lingering past of asbestos we chose Asbestos, Quebec, which embodies the *here* of the everywhere of asbestos. Asbestos, Quebec, besides proudly wearing the mineral's name, is home to the Jeffrey Mine. It is the largest asbestos mine in the world and, as Jessica van Horssen puts it in her study of the town's history, 'the source of the community's pride and sorrow, success and decline' (2016, 15): an extractivist pharmakon. While the history of Asbestos is in many ways visible upon the surface of the town's contemporary configuration, its details bear pausing upon, as it is telling not only of the history of its mineral namesake but also of the broader trends in twentieth-century industrial development.

The Jeffrey Mine was opened in 1881 with merely fourteen men, expanding to become the world's leading producer of asbestos by 1896. During the early decades of the twentieth century, Asbestos, Quebec, was providing up to 80 percent of the global asbestos supply. The Second World War saw an increase in the demand for asbestos, and by the war's end the community of Asbestos was beginning to feel concern toward the health hazards of the material. In 1949 the workers of the Jeffrey Mine went on a five-month strike, demanding better health conditions. The strike choked up the global supply of asbestos, which has led historians to view it 'as a turning point in the history of the working class in Canada' (Van Horssen 2016, 14). Yet despite the increasingly deteriorating health of the townspeople of Asbestos throughout the first half of the twentieth century, there were no officially recorded asbestos-related deaths in Canada until the 1970s. This was largely due to an aggressive campaign of misinformation with regard to the detrimental effects of asbestos on human health funded by JM, the company running the Jeffrey Mine. In the 1950s JM hired medical professionals to attribute the lung cancer which was common among the mine workers to their cigarette-smoking habits, and to smuggle up to seventy lungs of deceased miners into the United States in order to study the relationship between asbestos and cancer in anonymity, and without notifying or compensating the victims' families (Van Horssen 2016, 112). As asbestos particles breached the boundaries of the workers' lungs, the corporation breached national borders to obscure the visibility of its toxicity.

In 1975, the workers in the Jeffrey Mine went on strike one more time. This time, however, it was not to demand better health conditions but rather job security, as JM had begun to lay off workers due to the dwindling global demand for asbestos, following the revelations of its molecular structure and toxicity. This episode is a stark instance of the generally non-linear industrial history of asbestos. In a complete reversal of their protest a generation earlier, 'as the industry rapidly declined around them, Jeffrey Mine workers became its biggest advocates, minimizing the risks it posed and using their own bodies to show they were unaffected by asbestos-related disease' (van Horssen 2016, 15). Ultimately JM filed for bankruptcy and sold the mine in 1983, and from then until 2012 the town received subsidies from the local and federal governments in order to keep the Jeffrey Mine operational. Although the domestic use of asbestos in Canada and its heretofore primary importers in the West had ceased by the 1980s, the Jeffrey Mine only stopped extraction in 2012, having exported the ore to developing nations, chief among them India.

For decades Canada 'exploited its generally positive international image to cast shadows over medical reports proving the dangers of asbestos' in order to be able to generate continued demand for asbestos and 'sell the mineral to developing countries, where workers and other citizens were neither adequately informed about the risks nor protected from them' (van Horssen 2016, 13). As Kathleen Ruff (2017) shows in her report on the events leading up to the Canadian ban of asbestos, the Canadian government founded, and until 2009 funded, the Asbestos Institute, later renamed the Chrysotile Institute to avoid any negative associations. The institute bribed scientists into publishing misleading research in an attempt to undermine the scientific consensus around the dangers of asbestos. Furthermore, in 2006 the Canadian government instrumentalised their perceived international goodwill to play a key role, alongside Russia, in suppressing an amendment to the Rotterdam convention on harmful materials to include asbestos, which in itself would not impose a ban, but merely require 'exporting countries to obtain Prior Informed Consent from any country to which they wish to export the hazardous substance' (Ruff 2017, 4), something so insufficient for public health yet deemed excessive by Canadian asbestos exporters.

The continuation of asbestos mining in Quebec was a public health hazard worldwide, and although its termination depended on a decision made by the local government, it was instigated by an international advocacy campaign spearheaded by the anti-asbestos movements of the importing countries, such as the Ban Asbestos Network of India. Ordinarily to achieve a ban on asbestos, asbestos victims organisations and trade unions would take a leading role in campaigns. Quebec and Canada, however, presented a special case where there were no asbestos victims organisations and the trade unions were in fact part of the pro-asbestos lobby, advocating on behalf of the mine workers, who were 'as they saw it, fighting for their jobs and the survival of their community' (Ruff 2017, 3). The efforts to ban asbestos mining in Canada had to appeal instead to the progressive values of 'international solidarity, human rights, scientific integrity, and worker health' as aimed at the Canadian people by the world trade union movement, most prominently Indian asbestos victims, trade unionists and activists, and as undersigned by numerous respected international and Quebecois scientists (3). Ultimately, the battle was won in the court of public opinion, which had for decades been skewed by government-funded misinformation. In 2012 the Jeffrey Mine

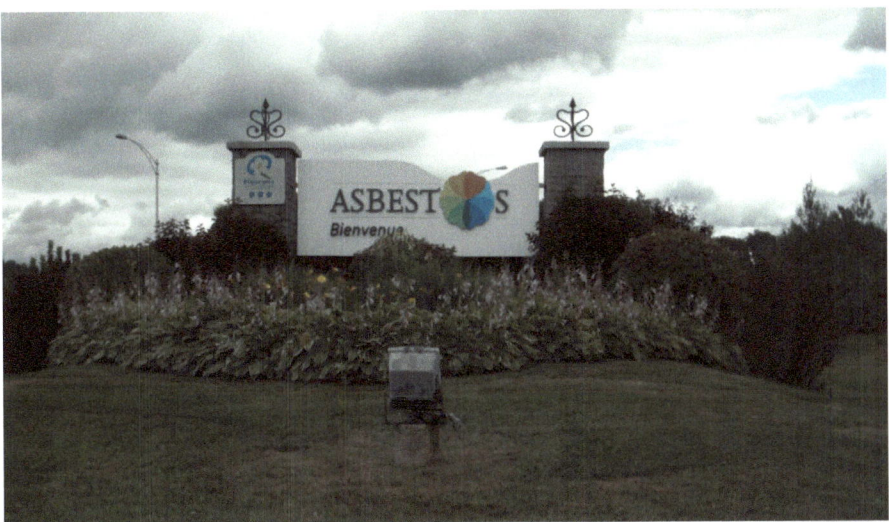

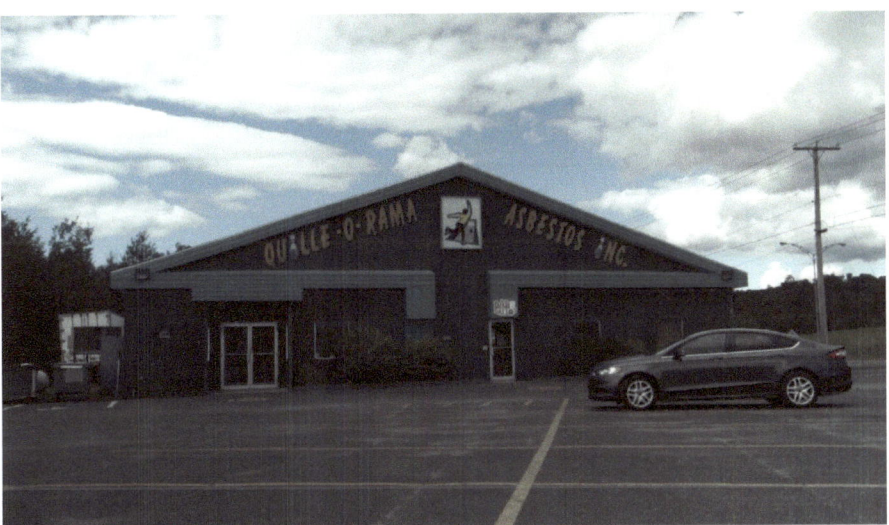

Fig 3. and Fig. 4. Stills from *Asbestos* (2016), Sasha Litvintseva and Graeme Arnfield.

was due a loan from the Conservative government in order to continue operations for another twenty years, a decision which was cancelled later that year with the election of Parti Québécois in Quebec and the Liberal party in federal government, both parties having run campaigns that promoted the asbestos ban. The Jeffrey Mine was immediately shut down and asbestos was officially banned in Canada by 2018.

There are not many images of the town available online. In preparing for the shoot I had to trust that I will be able to find visual traces of this history that will be as rich in contradiction as the material itself. When first arriving in Asbestos by car from Montreal, I headed for the site of the Jeffrey Mine, now viewable from an observation platform. It is hard for images to mediate the sheer scale of the gaping two-kilometre-wide cavity of the former mine. Spiralling levels large enough for mining trucks to drive down register as steps one could walk up; trees on the opposite side of the crater appear as but moss. Standing on the edge of the crater in tempestuous wind, it is impossible not to feel the enormity and longevity of the scar upon this landscape – and far beyond it. Driving back into town, I see more and more of the history reveal itself in the details. The name of the town, itself a reminder of the misguided pride and hope that is characteristic of the history of this 'magic mineral', is prominently displayed on flowerbeds, lamppost flags and signage (fig. 3). The laundromat, the hospital and the bowling alley all sport the word 'asbestos' in their names (fig. 4). Most strikingly to me, the supermarket parking lot wall is covered by a mural celebrating the mining history of the town. The mural features turn of the last century miners with grey skin, various municipal buildings and even a 'Cinema Asbestos', which I sadly could not find in the town itself. The mural is also extremely run down, fading and peeling off, having been painted at an indeterminate time prior to 2012 and not kept up since. Yet, importantly, neither had it been painted over: the town owns the fact that it exists as a direct consequence of the presence of asbestos in the ground beneath it. Asbestos, Quebec *is* the *here* of the *everywhere* of asbestos.

There are many ways to shoot exterior scenes. Shots could be static or moving, wide or close-ups, composed with the sky taking up the upper third of the screen, exactly half, or even the upper two thirds. One could use a tripod and pan or tilt the camera on an axis, or create a tracking shot on a dolly and track, or even from a moving vehicle. One could collect detailed close-ups or experiment with oblique angles. Yet the more time I spent exploring every street of the town, the more it became clear to me that there was only one way to shoot Asbestos, Quebec. The town is an immovable dot on the map when compared to the journey of its mineral product. To accentuate the situated heaviness of the marks of the history of asbestos upon its surface, as well as its own localised singularity, I opt to shoot only from a tripod. The static shots are an attempt to say *this* is *here*. This flowerbed decorating the word 'Asbestos' is in this place. It could not be anywhere else. I frame the images as wide as possible in order to allow for the widest possible array of incidental detail to make it into each shot, providing lived context for the more recognisable marks of asbestos. I also aim to foreground not only the aspects of the town that make it singular, but also those that mark it as one of countless small North American industrial towns and suburbs. I shoot the residential streets, their architecture and layout so familiar (to a non-North American like myself) from a wide corpus of cinema. Here, the streets are quiet in the daytime as, after the shutting down of the mine, most of the residents have to commute to work elsewhere. I shoot the new small industries springing up on the outskirts of town, such as the (humorously named) 'Beton Asbestos' cement plant. I frame the decaying industrial machinery discarded on the edge of the mine in the same way that I frame the buildings of the new industries – straight on and slightly from below – to underline the fact that they both equally occupy *this* present moment. Meanwhile, the way the angle makes the foreboding and changeable cloudy sky more prominent foregrounds the transience of each such moment.

Working with the found footage, in contrast, by definition means working with a multitude of temporalities that coexist within the space of the archive. My collaborator Graeme Arnfield sourced all of the found footage that appears in *Asbestos* from the decentralised archives of YouTube. YouTube, as it has evolved in its contemporary form, is as much an archive of pre-existing moving image material, including the digitised versions of established film archives – many of which have their own channels – as it is a broadcasting platform that has engendered numerous new genres of moving images. In other words, on YouTube a 1990s music video and a 1950s PSA film, which would have otherwise only been available through the Prelinger Archives, coexist alongside video genres that are specific to YouTube itself, such as a vlog or a haul video. Asbestos video content turned out to be no exception to this. Our choice to focus specifically on YouTube was due to the way in which all these different types of material are placed alongside one another without any central organising cataloguing system, the way it would be in a traditional archive: they are only organised by an algorithm that places them in relation to each other. In the dispersed media hosted on this rhizomatic platform we sought traces of the globally dispersed toxic material. To accomplish this, Arnfield searched the keywords 'asbestos', 'asbestos removal', 'asbestos decontamination' not only in English, but also in French, German, Russian, etc., and he also followed the trails of the algorithm's suggested videos, which led him to find asbestos removal videos from an ever-increasing number of locations. In contrast with the localised specificity of Asbestos, Quebec, these videos testified to the ongoing global persistence of asbestos – and of the effort to undo the toxic history of its use.

Arnfield initially collated many tens of hours of footage of asbestos removal (although several of them were many-hours-long single shot videos by one

Swedish asbestos removal worker, who filmed every job he did and none of whose videos had a single view). True to the logic of YouTube, the material ranged from formal instructional videos to vlogs shot by workers wearing GoPro cameras on their heads. The latter had been made specifically for YouTube (even if, as it transpires, no one really watches them). What was most striking about the set of videos, however, was the array of film and video formats: from 16mm to magnetic tape to HD. This plethora of different media formats was a visible testament to the durational nature of the global efforts of asbestos decontamination, a process that the quality of these images shows to have been unfolding for many decades, from the early days of asbestos regulation in the 1970s to the present day (figs. 5-6). In choosing the specific videos to use in the film we were initially guided by a desire to represent as many media formats, and therefore historical moments, as possible. In order to be able to begin to find and single out videos from the many hours of clips, we were also guided by an attempt to find similarities among them on a granular level. We gathered shot after shot in which the workers were seen to be laboriously putting on protective equipment and meticulously wrapping entire houses in plastic. The bodies of the workers were visually accessible only as mediated by the hazmat suits that covered them, just as they were physically mediated by them to the toxic atmospheres they occupied. During the practice of removal the potential for submicroscopic asbestos fibres to pass from stable to airborne warrants

Perception: Asbestos 85

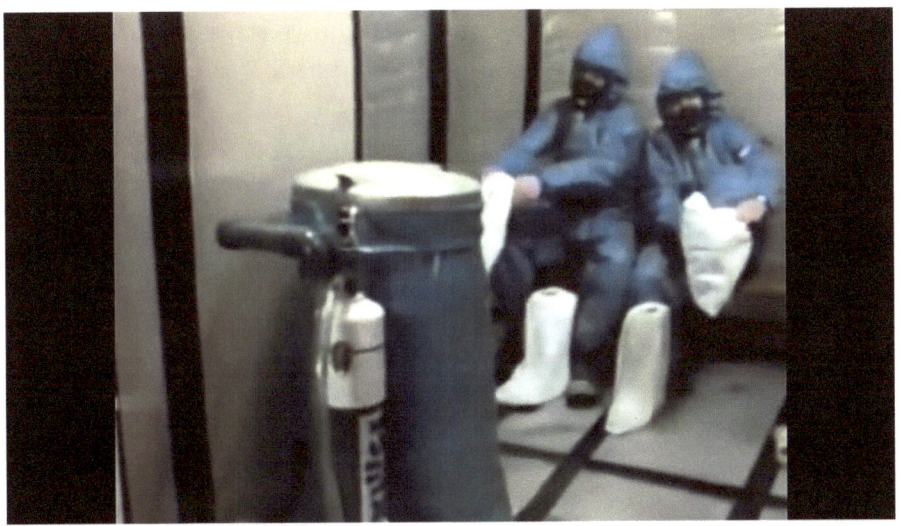

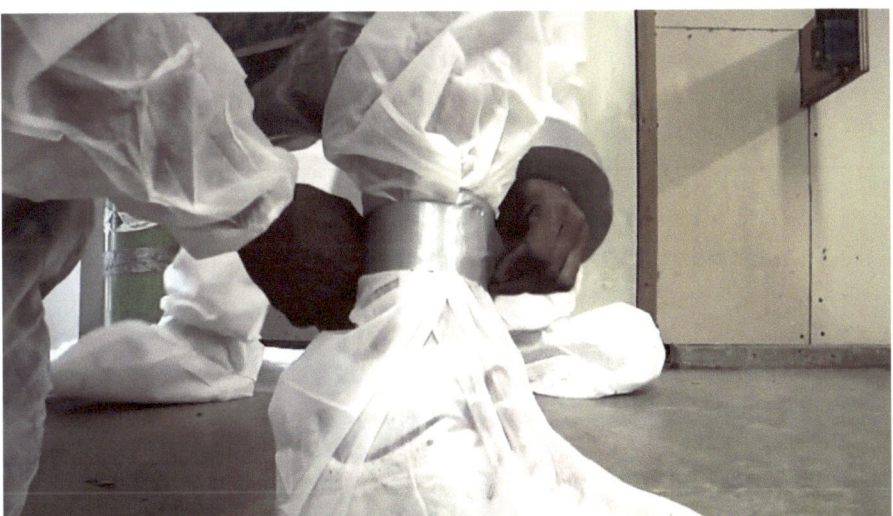

Fig. 5 and Fig. 6. Stills from *Asbestos* (2016), Sasha Litvintseva and Graeme Arnfield.

the deployment of a highly-material infrastructure. In the footage of removal this material infrastructure of protective layers of plastic becomes a visual manifestation of airborne asbestos fibres, an indexical trace of an atmosphere that is imperceptible but nevertheless visibly toxic.

Sitting down to edit the film together, Arnfield and I had to decide how to build the relationship of the found material to the shot material. In this type of non-fiction filmmaking the film is written entirely in the edit, so finding the right path for the sequence and the build-up of images, sounds and scenes is everything. We could have edited the film chronologically, either from the point of view of historical development – from the mining to the removal – or from the point of view of the provenance of the clips themselves – from older celluloid material, to the contemporary material, including my own. Yet there is no such linearity to the history of the industrial use of asbestos. Beginning to remove asbestos from the existing architecture in order to counteract the history of its extraction did not mean that the extraction and use had themselves stopped – the two contradictory processes have been going on side by side for decades. The two types of footage are thus not edited into a linear causal narrative but exist side by side. The film continuously fluctuates between the footage of removal and the footage I shot in Asbestos, Quebec. To contrast the consistent exteriors of the latter, we chose only interior videos of removal. To contrast the slow and ponderous wide shots almost devoid of people, we chose removal shots that were dynamic, embodied and full of bodies. The final film is an attempt to articulate the oscillating poles of asbestos, at once local and global, situated and dispersed, static and mobile, latent and current, imperceptible and material. Our aim was to hold all these multifaceted dimensions of asbestos in balance, while letting its various aspects be visibly different in a way that was only possible as a result of a collaboration between two filmmakers pursuing their own approaches in parallel.

The process of geological filmmaking does not stop at a finished film. The process is initiated by a theoretical question – and the making of the film involves a practical investigation that attempts to provide the answer to this question. The final step in the methodology of geological filmmaking is thus the making of a theoretical claim on the basis of the insights gained in the making of the film. Here, I was approaching the question of imperceptibility in the ecological crisis through the impossible practical challenge of optically mediating submicroscopic material. Having now made the film, I am able to argue that the aesthetic challenge posed by the imperceptible aspects of the ecological crisis is not so much about making the invisible visible but rather about engaging with, and accounting for, the existing points of connection between human bodies and systems, and the seemingly imperceptible objects of study. What is made visible in the optically-captured images that make up the film is not asbestos itself but the practices and infrastructures it necessitates and leaves in its wake, the chain reaction that is triggered by its extraction from the ground. In an attempt to tackle an imperceptible material through a visual medium, what comes into sharp relief is the contact zone between the material and its use. This realisation is key, as it is precisely that contact zone that needs examining and renegotiating. The inevitable shift of focus to the environments, bodies and practices that have been engendered or transformed by asbestos ultimately points to the necessity of their inclusion in any discussion of toxic materials.

Asbestos the mineral and *Asbestos* the film demonstrate that the human does not just touch the nonhuman and that culture does not just touch nature, but that the boundaries between all those spheres are porous in the entangled and reciprocal co-emergence of the socio-economic and the geologic, and of our mortal bodies and environments. The medium of film provides here a perceptual framework within which to contemplate these inextricable connections across all scales: from the molecular to the planetary, from the immediate to the stretches of deep time. I will thus further propose that asbestos the mineral and *Asbestos* the film in their respective ways traverse the boundaries of inside and outside. Those boundaries shift in scale from individual cells to the skin that forms the outer boundary of our bodies, from our skin to the outer skin of the protective hazmat suits, from the bodies to the walls, from interiors to exteriors, from the local to the global, and, last but not least, from the screen to the optical nerve.

But can the image really be said to touch or penetrate the eye, or the eye to touch the image? The idea of haptic cinematic images was developed by Laura U. Marks, who asserted that 'in haptic *visuality* the eyes themselves function like organs of touch' (Marks 1998, 332). As Thomas Elsaesser and Malte Hagener elaborate, theories of cinematic haptic perception 'could be seen as a reaction or backlash against the "scopic regime" of previous theories (based on distance)' (2000, 10), highlighting instead 'the interplay, continuity, and transition between … the film and the viewer' (130). While such proximity, mutuality and continuity between viewer and film are in principle an apt avenue for a cinematic exploration of a haptic encounter with a boundary-breaching material, I would argue that it is in fact the very gap between the metaphorical touch of the cinematic image and physical touch that lends itself as a tool for a discussion of the hapticity of asbestos. The touch of the image does not involve physical contact and the touch of asbestos is imperceptible. It is in this sense that a cinematic experience could be a useful instrument for thinking through a haptic encounter with a toxic atmospheric threat, an encounter which is not mutual in the way that physical touch between two solid bodies of comparable size is. As Barad interrogates in her essay 'On Touching', which complicates the way touch is understood in classical physics, 'what would it mean to acknowledge that responsibility extends to the insensible as well as the sensible, and that we are always already opened up to the other from the "inside" as well as the "outside"?' (2012, 218). In considering touch from the perspective of both outside boundaries and their breaching, the perceptible and the imperceptible, what Barad highlights is the responsibility that comes with vulnerability: 'the sense of exposure to the other is crucial and so is the binding obligation that is our vulnerability' (218). The mutuality of the type of touch that is immaterial in the way of cinematic images, or imperceptible and penetrating in the way of asbestos, arises not between viewer and film, or body and toxic atmosphere, but rather between responsibility and vulnerability triggered by the encounter.

Thinking back to the history of Asbestos, Quebec, the complexity of the reciprocity of vulnerability and responsibility comes into play. In trying to defend the mine in the name of their community despite the evident danger to their own health, 'the people of Asbestos entered into a relationship of mutual exchange with the land, shaping it and being shaped by it' (van Horssen 2016, 15-16). It was a reciprocal double bind with the toxic material that both threatened their community and 'gave their community purpose' (10-11). Yet the double bind between the town and the toxic material resulted in a violent equilibrium of continued extraction, and it was only in encountering the vulnerability to the toxic material *in another*, in this case an international community of asbestos victims' advocates, that change could be brought about. The community of bodies sharing a toxic atmosphere was not just limited by the outer boundary of the town of Asbestos but included the whole of the developing world.

The negotiation of the boundary between inside and outside, and of the mutuality of vulnerability and responsibility, triggered by the toxic hapticity of asbestos extends from the breaching of the boundary of a single cell by a submicroscopic shard of asbestos to the spatial and temporal qualities of asbestos as it disperses around the world. It also extends to the way asbestos projects itself into the future. Once removed from buildings, asbestos and asbestos-infused materials are most commonly buried in hazardous-waste landfill sites. However, this practice does not take away from the potential toxicity of the material and remains safe only as long as the deposits remain undisturbed. Indeed, asbestos removal confirms that there is no 'outside' in which to deposit toxic materials. This realisation has broader implications for environmental sustainability, as being always and already an embedded part of the environment means there is no 'outside' to either vulnerability or responsibility. There is no transcending our material environment, so when it comes to cohabiting alongside existing toxic materials and imagining a future among environmental degradation already underway, a liveable future will not be imposed on the environment from the outside or be built despite it – it can only emerge from within it.

A final note on the passage of time, as we conclude the engagement with the town of Asbestos, Quebec. In the late stages of my redrafting of this manuscript in

October 2020, the town voted to change its name from Asbestos to Val-des-Sources. There were a number of names in contention. One of these was Phénix: asbestos-themed in the sense of being inflammable, industrial-failure-themed in the sense of rising from the ashes. Some of the names were the anonymous sounding Larochelle and Trois-Lacs. It is curious that, ultimately, in moving away from the descriptive 'Asbestos', the township nevertheless went for the equally descriptive 'Valley of Resources'. This choice seems to embody the enduring ambivalence of the town's relationship to its history: on the one hand going through the (expensive) trouble to rename the town in the realisation of the harm of the negative association, but at the same time being proud of being a valley of resources and wanting to hold on to that part of its identity. With the name change many other visible changes are likely to follow: the 'Asbestos' signage and flags will be taken off, the cement plant, bowling alley and other local businesses are likely to be renamed, perhaps even the mural will be painted over. The cavity of the mine will of course remain (although there are discussions of turning it into an outdoor velodrome). Many of the things I filmed as a way to visually narrate the history of the town will disappear, emphatically highlighting the transient nature of the moment in which I filmed them. And, with that, the film will no longer be a record of *this* moment but rather of *that* past moment: the summer of 2016. After all, this is all we ever have access to: every gesture, creative or activist, is a gesture

Perception: Asbestos 93

within its specific moment. Whether or not this gesture remains meaningful over a prolonged period of time, each new moment that comes will continue to necessitate further action.

Asbestos Time: Material Debt and Unintended Consequences

My collaborator and I spent many days reviewing all the found footage material of asbestos removal. Late one evening, after beginning to lose the ability for detailed attention after many hours of work, we came across the 1980s documentary whose tape had been damaged, resulting in distorted colours, and were immediately startled into attention. We watched its entire hour-long duration with bated breath. There was no question that a number of scenes from the footage would end up being pivotal moments in the film, as it served as a powerful reminder of a key aspect of cinematic temporality. From the beginning of film history the fragility and impermanence of the material carrier, from celluloid to magnetic tape to digital files (no less material than the other two), has been what defines and delimits the future of a given film. Early cinematic nitrate stock, for example, was made using camphor and nitrocellulose – materials which are, famously, extremely flammable, but also very difficult to store – eventually disintegrating into a sticky gel and thus mutating beyond the ability to retain the images it carries given enough time. For Cubitt, however, this process is not to be understood merely as destruction, but as an 'evolution of a new

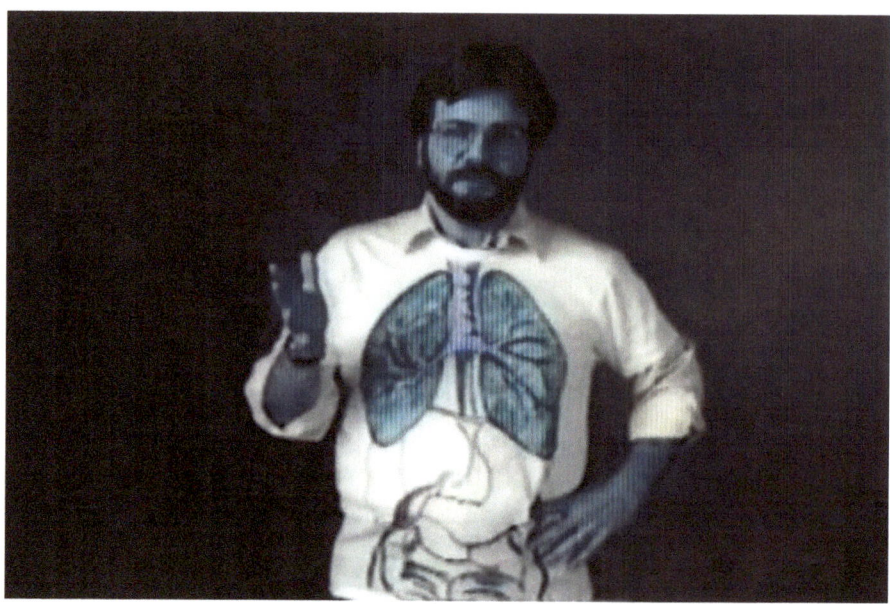

Fig. 7. Still from *Asbestos* (2016), Sasha Litvintseva and Graeme Arnfield.

artefact from the old' (Cubitt 2017, 2). In their materiality all moving images are subject to entropy, but the resultant change is not simply an erasure of a past communication, which would mean privileging the content over the materiality or a complex understanding of cinematic temporality. It carries the potential to communicate across time, beyond the original intent of the human creators. What is it, then, that the damaged video footage used in *Asbestos* helps us perceive?

Some of the aged and decayed images are of once cutting-edge laboratory optical technology and stand in contrast to the crisp HD images I shot of the ageing and decaying industrial machinery at the mine. The optical technology from the 1980s depicted in the corrupted images is now out of date, reminding us that the contemporary HD images may themselves become entirely unreadable due to a future switch in file formats. The compromised images are still able to communicate their content, but their damaged material support communicates the complexities of asbestos temporality with added nuance and accuracy. The temporality of asbestos embodies a contradiction surrounding (un)certainty. On the one hand, it is defined by unintended consequences: asbestos' fall from grace followed millennia of it being treated as a 'magic mineral', serving as but one example of the unplanned toxic consequences of extractive capitalism, alongside rising CO_2 in the atmosphere as a result of the burning of fossil fuels. On the other hand, when looked at from the point of view of asbestos' encounter with biological matter, its temporality is defined by a *certain* future: in the piercing of a cell a process is triggered that makes some aspects of the future guaranteed.

In the distorted images of the corrupted magnetic tape the damage to the surface of the physical carrier of the moving images is primarily made visible in their distorted colours. In one of the scenes the presenter speaks directly to the camera about the insidiousness of the delay to the deadly effects of asbestos. His skin colour bright blue, he says: 'I sometimes wish that when we humans were exposed to asbestos, that somehow or another we would turn green or blue immediately, so that we'd know we'd had the asbestos exposure and possibly could do something about it' (fig. 7). What he wishes had been possible in order for asbestos exposure to be detectable before its certain yet deferred effects appear with the passage of time, has with retroactive irony in fact happened through the effect of entropy on the footage. In other words, the degradation of the materiality of the tape that carries the image manifests upon the body of the presenter the deferred effects that asbestos exposure would have upon the lungs of which he speaks. These compromised images communicate the two sides of asbestos temporality: in preserving the ability to relay their content, the images attest to the original intentions of their creators, a temporality imposed on them from the outside, just like the extraction and industrial use was imposed on asbestos. In their degradation, in turn, the images attest to the temporality that emanates from within their materiality and thus communicates the latent temporality inherent to asbestos. What the damaged images from the documentary reveal is that these two modes of relating to the future are not contradictory, but rather that human agency or intention, as invested into the content of the images or the extraction of asbestos, is but one factor among a host of material agencies, such as those manifest in the entropy that ravishes cinematic images over time and in the specificities of the molecular structure of asbestos.

The dual temporal model of thinking through the non-contradiction of the unintended consequences of technoscience and extractive capitalism, and about the certain future of the unfolding of the specificities of matter, can be applied to thinking the ecological crisis more broadly. On the one hand, the force of the material agency of asbestos demonstrates that, as Yusoff suggests, durability within the ecological crisis will need to include 'understanding duration as a form of responsibility to the ongoing material and immaterial recombinations of matter that exceed social action' (2013, 211). On the other hand, it provides a culturally resonant reference point for the fallibility of technoscientific and industrial progress. In a 2017 article in *The Guardian* entitled 'The Death of Diesel: Has the One-time Wonder Fuel Become the New Asbestos?' (Forrest 2017), asbestos is used as an analogue of a newly failed promise. The logic of infinite growth implicit in capitalism and industrial progress craves magical and wondrous materials, which it requires as resources and leaves behind as waste. Yet the unintended consequences of materials such as asbestos (which causes deadly illness) and diesel (which was marketed and subsidised as a green alternative to petrol but turned out to be more toxic than regular fuel) have a markedly different relationship to futurity than that implied by the capitalist logic of infinite growth. Indeed, the capitalisation of nature and its unintended consequences have always gone hand in hand, as Friedrich Engels argues in *The Dialectics of Nature*, writing that 'each victory [over nature] in the first place brings about the results we expected, but in the second and third places it has quite different, unforeseen effects which only too often cancel the first' (1946, 291). For this reason 'we find that there still exists here a colossal disproportion between the proposed aims and the results arrived at, that unforeseen effects predominate, and that the uncontrolled forces are far more powerful than those set into motion according to plan' (291-2). His analysis is almost exactly contemporaneous with the very beginning of industrial mining of asbestos, being two years apart from the opening of the Jeffrey Mine. In the end, Engels attests, nature always 'takes its revenge' (291).

Yet despite initially seeming like unintended consequences, once the asbestos particles have entered the cells of the body or diesel exhaust along with other greenhouse gases have entered the atmosphere, some aspects of the future become guaranteed. From the perspective of the contemporary eco-critical discourse, it may not be suitable to think of this process through the framework of revenge, as this approach would anthropomorphically infuse the materials with vengeful intentionality. Rather, the deferred yet certain temporality of those materials could be considered from the perspective of the temporality of a debt repayment obligation. The reason debt provides a useful framework for thinking the certainty embedded in the temporality of materials and of nonhuman processes, is that it brings obligation and responsibility into the centre of the discussion. This includes an obligation to the past and a responsibility for the future. Framing environmental degradation through the concept of debt allows for a description of the temporality of such aspects of the ecological crisis as the finitude of natural resources, the fate of the already emitted CO_2 and the long-term storage of nuclear waste. Indeed, 'climate debt' is being widely used in the official discourse of climate change to differentiate between the responsibilities of developing and industrialised nations, wherein the industrialised nations have used up their emissions 'allowance' over the past two centuries and therefore 'owe' an emissions liability to the developing nations. This means 'this climate debt requires a cut in developed world emissions sufficiently far as to leave "room" under the overall limit for currently underdeveloped nations to expand their economies and mitigate the everyday emergency of their living standards' (Mirzoeff 2013, 832-3). Here 'climate debt' is understood as a technically repayable debt owed by one set of humans to another. I would go further to suggest that the very temporal condition of the ecological crisis can be thought of from the perspective of debt. Perhaps it can be thought of as a material debt: a debt taken out with the extraction and application, dissemination or burning of natural resources, its record stored in the molecular structure of toxic chemicals and greenhouse gases.

The temporal scale upon which this material debt unfolds can be at odds with contemporary political timeframes: the effects of CO_2 are measured in hundreds of years and half-lives of nuclear waste in hundreds of millennia, which makes the urgency of the crises seem deferred on the temporal scale of the parliamentary terms of party politics – becoming in effect a debt for and to future generations. Asbestos, with its relatively smaller time scale of effects upon the body measurable in decades, and the success of the activist movements to get it banned in an increasing number of countries, becomes a valuable tool for thinking through this temporal disjuncture. Through its toxicity asbestos brings embodied time into proximity with geological time; it also gives us a glimpse into the workings of the temporality of ecological debt and, with it, a glimpse into our deep future. That is to say, unless we begin to take account of and engage with the multiplicity of ecological temporalities now, the centuries that lie ahead will spell ecological catastrophe – the uncertain future of ecological collapse will certainly take place.

Yet the future is never written wholesale. Asbestos is but one example of a non-linear episode in the history of industrial progress. As such, it is a lesson in the potentially catastrophic unintended consequences of over-eager investments in particular resources or their uses. It also serves as further warning about the potential unintended consequences of the often hubristic attempts at hopeful techno-fixes to the ecological crisis. No once-and-for-all solution to the ecological crisis could be arrived at to which other unintended consequences would not arise. As we have seen in the deteriorated images from an out-of-date documentary on asbestos, certainty and uncertainty are not contradictory, and with the passage of time the intentional leaves as much of a trace as the unintended. A wholesale solution cannot be written into the future, but neither does it have to promise wholesale catastrophe: certain processes causing ecological devastation having already been set in motion does not mean that all hope is lost. It merely means that human agency will have to act in concert with the agency and material specificities of resources, landscapes and ecosystems, working with, not against, them, through an informed, continuous and ever-shifting step-by-step negotiation of the future.

CHAPTER 3

Depiction: Sinkholes

In many ways this chapter is its predecessor's mirror or inverse, the positive space to its negative space, the print to its woodcut. While in the previous chapter I explored the aesthetic challenges presented by the invisible aspects of the ecological crisis, this one shows that the trouble does not end with that which cannot be perceived, as the dominant visuality often actively obfuscates even the visible aspects of the crisis, as well as its causes and meanings. In this chapter I thus grapple with the formal and political questions surrounding the representation of nonhuman agency. Where in the previous chapter the dynamism of the geological was located in the molecular structure of a given material that was distributed around the world, here the dynamism of the geological is located in the situated transformation of a landscape under the influence of hydro-geological and anthropogenic forces. The politics of the porosity between humans and nonhumans, and between bodies and environments, is now manifested in the instrumentalisation of nonhuman entities used as tools of settler colonialism – and in their refusal to be complicit.

Methodologically, this chapter follows a similar path to the preceding one, beginning with a theoretical situation of its key question. This chapter was also developed in reciprocal conversation with the making of a film, *Salarium* (2017), which engages with its theoretical questions directly though filmmaking. The film confronts the transformation of the landscape of the Dead Sea shore in the West Bank through the appearance of thousands of sinkholes. Here, too, as in the rest of the project, the key focus is not on the geological entity of the sinkhole as such, but on the very intersection of human (social, economic, political, industrial, technological) and geophysical agencies. The filmmaking itself becomes a mode of participating in this intersection of agencies and processes, offering a direct material engagement with the world. A crucial insight from the practical filmmaking investigation pertains to an appreciation of the physical limits to the scope of one's intended actions. A major part of the methodology of geological filmmaking itself is that formal approaches cannot be premeditated but emerge through the unfolding process of engagement with the specificity of both the moving image medium and the nonhuman subject of the film. The practical filmmaking work thus provides an avenue for actively exploring what it means to be an engaged participant in perpetually unfolding processes, instead of imposing one's premeditated plan on them. These are valuable tools for the broader issues of living in and through the ecological crisis.

Nature Represents Itself?

In her essay 'No Representation without Colonisation? (Or, Nature Represents Itself)' (2015), Astrida Neimanis asks a provocative question: is it possible to represent nonhuman natures without simultaneously subjugating them? Applying Gayatri Chakravorty Spivak's (1988) work on the dangers of misrepresenting subaltern subjects to the representation of nonhuman natures, Neimanis suggests that while we 'fear that a lack of representation will lead to further incursion and devastation, in which we are thus complicit', representational impulses, no matter how well-meaning, risk leaving their object 'rendered passive and mute' (2015, 135-7). She elaborates that 'due to a Western mindset that perceives nature as only instrumental, a resource to be used, or a silent backdrop, non-human natures suffer many harms at the hands of such-thinking humans, and thus seem to demand that we speak for them' (139), yet we risk perpetuating some of these same forms of violence in the process of speaking *for* them. The dilemma applies to representation both in the mimetic sense of representing through an artistic medium, and political and legal representation in the sense of advocating *on behalf of* someone or something. As a possible way out from this bind Neimanis draws on the work of Karen Barad to argue for a representation without representationalism. In her critique of representationalism Barad (2007) foregrounds that this approach assumes the pre-existence of two distinct entities, representations and things to be represented, that are divided and mediated by yet another assumed and separate entity – a knowing subject. She contends that no such assumptions of *a priori* existence or separation can be made, and that engaging with the world in order to know it plays a role in the emergence of the world.

One of the most egregious examples of contemporary representationalist visualisations of the human impact on the planet are those that attempt to make visible the otherwise ungraspable immensity of the crisis by adopting a planetary perspective and scale. Such images rely on what Donna Haraway (1988) critiqued as the God's-eye-view, a disembodied gaze whose incorporeal perspective erases the experience of creaturely immersion in the world (Alaimo 2017, 90-92). By letting the viewer enjoy a supposedly neutral position outside the depicted systems and processes, the viewer is not implicated in them, either as a participant in the devastation or as a potential victim of its consequences. The comprehensive and schematic representation of the earth in such images also implies mastery over it, further replicating the violent objectifying logic that has perpetuated the crisis. A further political point arises in examining the technological underpinning of such images: planetary scale visualisations rely on a vast network of satellites and are therefore deeply embedded in the military-state-corporate apparatus (Demos 2017). Not only are such images produced by technologies enabled by this apparatus, but the universalising and undifferentiated sweep of human activity they depict on a planetary scale works to obstruct the differentiated responsibility of specific corporate and state entities, implying that it is the work of humanity as a whole. In other words, the military-state-corporate apparatus that powers the images that supposedly allow the ecological crisis to be 'seen' and therefore named is the very actor that is being absolved of responsibility by the totalising aesthetics of such images. This absolving makes the ecological crisis look like the work of humanity as a whole, thus obfuscating the origin of the responsibility.

A key point here is that representationalist images have a capacity to obfuscate, as much as to make intelligible, further undermining the possibility that they may be used as instruments of advocacy. Deliberate or otherwise, visual representations that obfuscate the nature, causes or stakes of the ecological crisis are conceptualised by Nicholas Mirzoeff (2014) as the Anthropocene visuality: the dominant visuality of capitalism, imperialism and industrialism over the past two centuries, where visuality is understood as the visualisation of history by a certain authority. To demonstrate how this figures throughout the art history of modernity, he uses Monet's painting *Impression Sun Rising* (1873) of the smog-covered port of La Havre, which, by rendering industrial air pollution as beautiful, naturalises and aestheticises it, and thus creates 'an anaesthetic to the actual physical conditions' (2014, 223). In this sense the complicit visual regime is one of the very forces that perpetuates the ecological crisis, for it blinds us to its reality and thus precludes mobilisation toward mitigating it. Ultimately, Mirzoeff calls for a countervisuality that would work against the *concealment* that defines the majority of contemporary cultural productions and that would claim 'the right to see what there is to be seen and name it as such: a planetary destabilization of the conditions supportive of life' (230). I would argue that it is crucial that any such countervisuality does not counter concealing with a mere revealing, but rather with an attempt to generate alternatives to representationalism.

In the very first instance it is necessary to account for the fact that 'nature – in the most expansive sense – represents itself all the time' (Neimanis 2017, 150). Imagining the non-representationalist possibilities for imaging the ecological crisis thus must include, as Susan Schuppli (2016) proposes, the imaging capacities of the damaged environments themselves. As an example Schuppli uses the Deepwater Horizon oil spill, where the oil molecules released by the spill into the Gulf of Mexico began interacting with the surface molecules of water in order to produce large-scale moving images of rainbow-coloured patterns. Oil's capacity to behave in this way is an inherent feature of its molecular materiality: the relationality of oil molecules is such that their density can vary, making a thicker or thinner film on the surface of the seawater and thus modulating the diffraction of light. Schuppli suggests that the oil spill produces 'an iridescent image of creeping dread: a horror film, in effect', thus also participating in the 'production of a new form of cinema organised by the found footage of "nature" itself' (2016, 191-3). A visual event thus occurs 'in which images move beyond their accepted role as representations of events, but are themselves an integral part of the unfolding action' (191). Schuppli argues further that 'the aesthetic agency of such damaged ecologies [is] fully capable of self-representation both before the law and as environmental media systems' (2020, 300). Understanding the behaviour of an oil spill in moving-image-making terms already offers a countervisuality to that driven by representational human-made images, generating a geo-photo-graphic (in the literal translation of earth-light-writing) condition, whereupon images that do not require human eyes are created as part of the rearrangements of molecular matter.

Where does this leave a human attempt to undertake non-representationalist image making? As Neimanis explicates, nature representing itself does not resolve but rather recasts the problem of representation: 'it is no longer primarily an ontological question (is representation possible?), but a decidedly ethical and political one', namely 'with what sort of responsibilities and accountabilities will we take up its pen?' (2015, 150). The formulation 'its pen' is key as it would be fallacious to imagine that humans have 'a pen' that is all their own – and not rooted in nonhuman natures. Representation without representationalism would thus need to take as its point of departure the inseparability of natureculture. The nonhuman within natureculture already represents itself as it overspills with agency that precedes and exceeds the human, and for humans there can be no speaking for nature, only speaking from inside natureculture. Barad's offering as an alternative to representationalism is agential realism, a performative onto-epistemological framework that aims at knowing the world by intra-acting with it from within. In her words, 'unlike representationalism, which positions us above or outside the world we allegedly merely reflect on, a performative account insists on understanding thinking, observing, and theorizing as practices of engagement with, and as part of, the world in which we have our being' (2007, 133). A performative approach 'takes account of the fact that knowing does not come from standing at a distance and representing but rather from *a direct material engagement with the world*' (49). Obfuscating and revealing aside, this is the foundation for a non-representationalist cinematic strategy that is at the core of geological filmmaking: a direct material engagement with the world.

Salarium does not set out to represent its nonhuman subject – the sinkholes decimating the Dead Sea shore – or even to represent the way in which human and geologic agencies converge in them: its primary aim was to be a means through which to engage with the landscape. If no prior separation can be assumed to exist between representations and entities represented, the images thus produced can be claimed to be mere manifestations of that situated material engagement. Film becomes a means of interacting with the material specificity of a given environment; of probing what is possible, which requires an openness to finding out something new about both the subject of the film and its medium. The filmmaking engagement with the landscape also actively aims to counter the visuality driven by the God's eye view from nowhere, and work toward developing a visual language that maintains a commitment to a situated and embodied way of knowing the world. The sinkholes initially attracted my attention as a potential subject for a film in the way that they actively intervened in the landscape: the sinkholes are both producer and product of the landscape's ongoing transformation. As their agency changes the consequent treatment of the landscape by undermining the possibility of its continued habitation, while also being their own visual trace, can the sinkholes be thought to represent themselves?

Sinkholes: Life and Nonlife, Surface and Depth

In October 2003, Eli Raz was walking on the Dead Sea shore not far from the Ein Gedi kibbutz. Eli, a scientist, has lived in the area since the 1970s, documenting its geological and biological transformation. On this day, he was out to document and measure a newly appeared sinkhole. Eli drove his jeep as close to the shoreline as he could, parked and walked down the muddy slope around where the soil meets the salty water. Since the 1980s, he has observed close to seven thousand sinkholes appear along the Dead Sea shore, rendering the natural shoreline all but inaccessible. In recent years, sinkholes have swallowed a number of people and destroyed numerous kibbutzim, tourist compounds, date orchards and roads. Once a sinkhole appears, others are soon to follow. The sinkholes form chains; they multiply and grow. Every solid surface on the shore harbours the potential to collapse. Young sinkholes are particularly treacherous as they can expand or multiply at any moment. As Eli was measuring a new sinkhole, the ground gave, and he fell in.

> Darkness. I assumed that I was covered inside the landslide, so I instinctively ploughed upwards as hard as I could. For a moment I thought that I have been blinded, or that this is how it is in the afterlife, but then light broke in through the thick dust and a large stain of blue sky appeared. On the top of a pile of soil and rocks, I acknowledged that I am alive, that I can see and I'm healthy and intact. When the dust sank down and settled below, the walls of the holes were visible, with the deep cracks in between the layers of dark soil. Climbing up the crumbling material was not an option. I was lost. (from Eli Raz's diary, written while stuck in a sinkhole)

In July 2017, my collaborator Daniel Mann and I are waiting for Eli at the roundabout near the entrance to the Ein Gedi kibbutz. After two days in the sinkhole, Eli was eventually rescued, and has dedicated the subsequent years to the study of the transforming landscape. We are meeting with Eli to hear about his experience

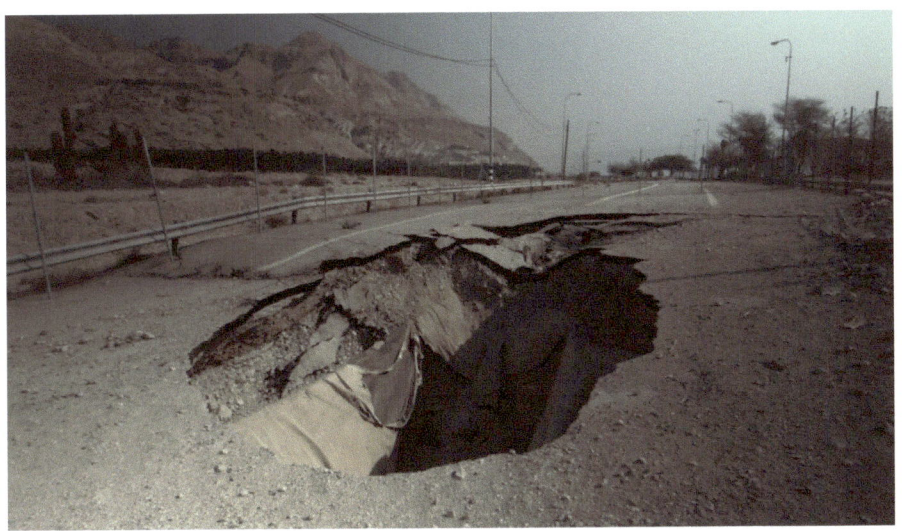

Fig 8. Still from *Salarium* (2017), Sasha Litvintseva and Daniel Mann.

of being stuck in the sinkhole, about his research into their causes, and, as importantly, to have him as our guide across the treacherous terrain, which would be too risky to attempt on our own as new sinkholes could appear anywhere at any time. Our meeting is scheduled for 5 am, to maximise being out on the shoreline before the direct sun starts to beat down on it and the temperatures rise above forty centigrade. Dawn is just about to crack when Eli appears.

As we walk along the shoreline, coming up to the edges of the existing sinkholes and gazing into their craters, me filming handheld and Mann recording sound, Eli narrates the geological causality of the sinkholes. For a sinkhole to appear, he explains, a cavity needs to have formed in the subterrain. On the Dead Sea shore, this happens when a subterranean salt layer dissolves. The level of the Dead Sea has been dropping steadily since the beginning of the twentieth century and at an increased pace in the past few decades. As the level of the Dead Sea fell, what used to be its seabed became exposed as its seashore. This newly exposed shore contains a thick layer of ancient salt deposits, formed under the sea, covered with a thin layer of topsoil and shaped by the sedimentation of geological debris travelling down the mountains into the sea. When this terrain remained submerged, the seawater's salinity meant it was unable to melt the salt deposits, but as it became exposed, the fresh water that came with winter flash floods penetrated through the dry topsoil and began to melt the salt deposits underneath. Over time, absences started to form in the volume of the terrain and the sinkholes appeared as the sudden collapse of the surface into the subterrain, exposing its depths and reconfiguring its surface (fig. 8).

Eli relishes the opportunity to be on camera. It is clear that it is not just our attention he hopes to hold, not just to us that he needs to convey his take on what is happening in the area: he is using the cinematic apparatus as a way to broadcast his views. There is a clear sense in his performative gusto that, had we been camera-less interested parties, he likely would not have agreed to meet with us. Eli is a scientist and he finds it easy to speak about the geological processes underpinning the appearance of sinkholes. What we know and are trying to get Eli to talk about, in order for this information to organically make it into the film through an existing speaking character, is the role of anthropogenic processes, and specifically the Israeli occupation, in the transformation of the landscape. In response to a number of direct questions, Eli concedes that the appearance of sinkholes and the rapid transformation of the landscape is a direct outcome of anthropogenic intervention into the hydro-geological cycles of the area and the resulting dropping of the level of the Dead Sea over the past half-century. What Eli will not elaborate on is the political dimension of the landscape's transformation, and yet that is the focus of our project.

Our collaboration is situated at the intersection of the political and the geological. Mann, an Israeli himself, had been aware of the Dead Sea sinkholes from local media, and was the one to bring up the subject with me in response to the issues I was concerned with, specifically the ability of geological formations to visually manifest the multiple human and nonhuman agencies acting upon them. His own research at the time was concerned with the use of habitual media in the Israel-Palestine conflict, and, with that, the impossibility of drawing solid boundaries between combat and the everyday. To *Salarium* he brought invaluable knowledge of the history and politics of the region, and the understanding of the use of means other than direct combat in fighting that particular war. Through our combined approaches, we conceived of the intersection of human and nonhuman processes unfolding on the Dead Sea shore as war being conducted by environmental means, or, in other words, the nonhuman landscape being instrumentalised as a tool of the occupation.

What Eli must know, but won't say, is that the dropping of the sea level is primarily affected by two factors. One of them is the overextraction of minerals from the West Bank shoreline by private Israeli companies; the other is the rerouting of water from the river Jordan in order to irrigate lands that were confiscated on the basis of claims of their prior non-cultivation. The two causes of the dropping of sea level can be examined from the perspective of what Elizabeth A. Povinelli calls geontopower, the governance of the separation of life and nonlife demanded and reaffirmed by 'extractive capital and its state allies' (2016, 44). She argues that the desert is seen by geontopower to reaffirm the distinction of life and nonlife and to stand 'for all things perceived and conceived as denuded of life – and, by implication, all things that could, with the correct deployment of technological expertise or proper stewardship, be (re)made hospitable to life' (16). In the Judean desert the question of life and nonlife has been particularly charged historically, as the posited absence of life in the area was used as a pretext by settler colonialism to justify the confiscation of Palestinian lands. In the Zionist imagination the desert could be transformed into flourishing arable lands, with Jewish settlements and kibbutzim using agricultural development as a colonial strategy of claiming territory. The rapid development of settlements meant that the scarce water sources available in the extreme desert terrain were circumvented to facilitate the irrigation of palm groves within Jewish settlements, leading to the dropping of the sea level and, consequently, the creation of sinkholes. The reliance on irrigation can be seen in the present lines of the landscape, where the date groves abandoned after being ridden with sinkholes appear as dried out hollow husks.

While the anthropogenic transformation of the Judean desert depended on the maintenance of the distinction between life and nonlife, the extraction of minerals from the Dead Sea implies a slippage in this distinction. The Dead Sea, with the salinity of 40% and rising, does not support any life other than bacterial: the mineral content of the sea acts to preclude the possibility of animal life. Meanwhile, the mineral mud being extracted and processed by Israeli companies along the

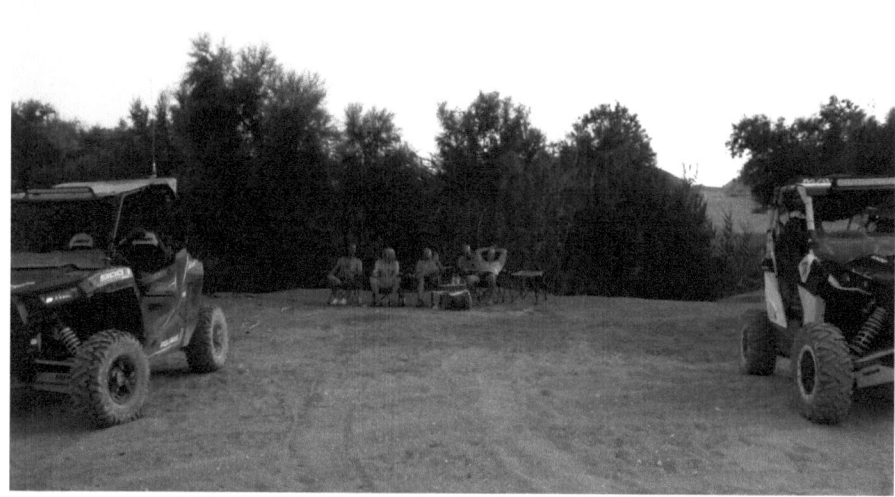

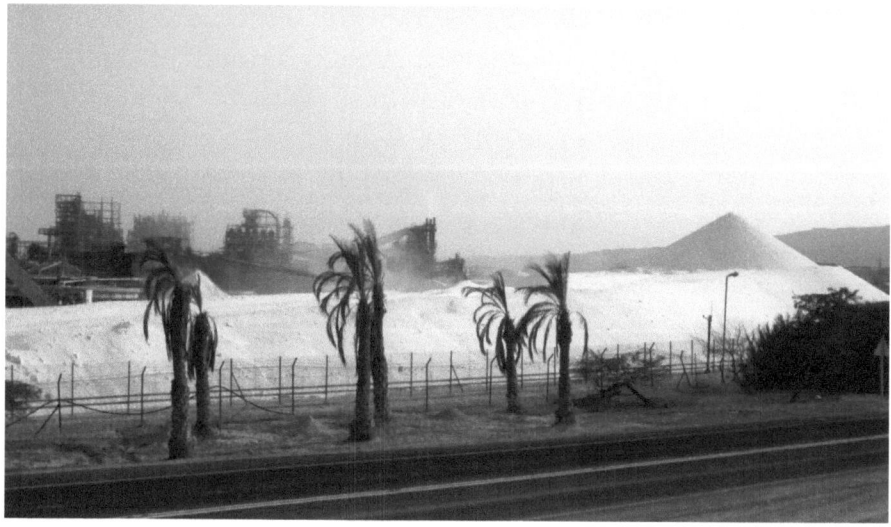

Fig 9. and Fig. 10. Stills from *Salarium* (2017), Sasha Litvintseva and Daniel Mann.

shoreline has been mythologised as having rare healing capacities. The dark subsoil being dug up by a booming cosmetics industry is a commodity that is being sold around the world with the promise of rejuvenation and good health. As Povinelli writes, the definition of life as self-directed biochemical activity only stands 'from the standpoint of the organism's so-called final membrane, ... a membrane that links and separates it from its environment. The final membrane of an individual human is usually thought of and experienced as skin' (2016, 52). She asserts that life and nonlife are only differentiated 'if the scale of our perception is confined to the skin' (56), and that we need only to shift the scale beyond the membrane of a single organism to perceive the mutual metabolism of the biological and the geological. The soil from the Dead Sea shore, the sinkholes and the bodies of people there and worldwide participate in a multiscalar bio-geological metabolism: while the Dead Sea mud is subsumed into the pores on the skin of people worldwide, its extraction facilitates the formation of pores in the surface of the Dead Sea landscape, which subsumes occasional individual human inhabitants as well as the possibility of continued human habitation. The extractive practices on the Dead Sea shore and the consequent appearance of sinkholes continuously breach the membrane between life and nonlife, organism and environment, across scales that are both local and global.

Despite the deathly heat, there is no shortage of tourists on the Dead Sea shore, rubbing the mud into their skin. Here, too, we find that the camera is what allows us access to the various people that occupy the landscape and to their takes on its transformation. Two Russian-Israeli women covered in mud rush to tell us about the landscape's energetic qualities. Five middle-aged settler men from Ma'ale Adumim, the largest Israeli settlement in the West Bank, who we unexpectedly encounter on a beach we expect to be populated by a group of off-the-grid recluses, are the first to strike up a conversation with us, albeit keeping it strictly to deserts and fresh water (fig. 9). On the same beach, a reclusive prophet is eager to tell us his religiously-informed take on environmental degradation, the first of all the above to acknowledge the devastation of the landscape. He is also the one to bring up the song 'In the year 2525', around which we subsequently structure the final scene of the film. Notably, there is a conspicuous absence of Palestinians anywhere near the shoreline.

While there are people and places to which the camera grants access, or indeed situations that precipitate directly in response to the presence of the camera, there are also those people and places to which the camera precludes access, appearing as a threat. When shooting the elevated static shot of the large factory (fig. 10), our presence with the camera immediately solicited a security van that swiftly moved us on. Soldiers, who are ubiquitous to the landscape, policing the border as well as beaches and gas stations, were not willing to interact upon sighting the camera. And yet it seemed crucial to foreground the presence of the anonymous citizen-soldier as emblematic of the specificity of the human-nonhuman relationship in this particular environment as always mediated by war. My collaborator Mann, whose previous film belonged to the genre of narrative fiction, therefore suggested using actors as soldiers, or indeed non-actors who had once been Israeli soldiers themselves and who wore their own former uniforms for the shoot. The interactivity of being able to direct (non)actors, a first for me, provided me with an opportunity for some of the most experimental camerawork in the film. Yet, importantly, the people who find themselves in this landscape, and the agricultural and extractive processes visibly unfolding here, are of course only a fraction of the story, and any attempt to filmically engage with the landscape's transformation will have to go far beyond what the people could reveal or what they try to hide. The film would need to find a way to incorporate agencies beyond the human as it is the sinkholes that are the story.

The perforated landscape of the Dead Sea shore is an example of a scenario in which, as put by Shela Sheikh, 'the environment itself becomes the medium through which violence is carried out' (2018, 450), as the extraction of resources from under the Palestinian territory and the introduction of agriculture as a method of the confiscation of land are methods of the occupation. In such a scenario, however, 'nature possesses a certain agency' (450), and the appearance of sinkholes, in turn, undermines the possibility of continuing with much of the agricultural and industrial activity that causes them. The sinkhole collapses two temporal and agential scales: on the one hand, the geological scale of gradual mineral sedimentation and erosion, and, on the other, the human historical scale of settler colonialism and resource extraction. More than just a surface interference, a sinkhole is also testament to unstable ground, such that the assumption of the existence of nature as a stable baseline to human activity, which has fuelled the environmental destabilisation in the area, can no longer be supported. The sinkhole's appearance, while being directly caused by anthropogenic changes to the geology of the area, itself directly interferes with the possibility of ongoing habitation or extraction. Eating away the palm groves, collapsing beneath the abandoned hotels and puncturing deep holes into the desert roads, sinkholes can perhaps be understood as the environment's refusal to be complicit with the slicing, cutting, fragmenting, cultivating, farming and confiscating of land and territory. Making the land uninhabitable in the future, the sinkhole appears as both visible symptom and active cause of this colonial project's failure to instrumentalise the environment. The geological here is far from the inert ideal object of the philosophy of old. The sinkhole is not merely a static consequence of human activity upon otherwise stable reserves; rather, it is both producer and product of the ongoing transformation of the naturecultural environment. Visually marking the landscape and materially disrupting the processes that led to their appearance, the sinkholes represent themselves.

In exploring how the agency of the sinkholes could be engaged through film, it is worth first confronting the role that visual representations of the area have played in their appearance. As the territory of the West Bank has been, and continues to be, highly politically contested, it is subject to meticulous cartographic representation. Yet these maps account only for the surface of the territory and not the resources underneath. As Eyal Weizman elaborates, 'two-dimensional maps, fundamental to the understanding of political borders, have been drawn again and again for the West Bank', yet 'each time they have failed to capture its vertical divisions' (2002, 2). Though control of the surface territory of the West Bank was given to the Palestinian Authority in 1995, Israel retained control over the subterranean volume of the terrain, thus allowing private companies in Israel to develop industry by the Dead Sea. The flatness of cartographic representation has fed into a conceptual disconnect around the continuity of the surface and depth of the landscape, which is exploited by the Israeli occupation. (The vertical dimensions that Israelis maintain control over in the West Bank further include airspace and the water and sewage systems.) As discussed above, the extractivist practices, which neglect the lines delineating Palestinian territory on the surface of the landscape and mine the resources underneath, are one of the causes of the dropping of the sea level and the resultant decimation of the Dead Sea shore by the sinkholes. Thus a causal link can be drawn between the surface level cartographic representation of the area and the appearance of the sinkholes. The sinkhole appears as the surface collapses into depth, and with that collapses the possibility of thinking territory merely in terms of surface: the volume of the terrain, the resources it holds and its geological agency are to be accounted for. Visually engaging with the agency of the sinkholes will thus be about visually establishing a relationship between the surface and the depth of the landscape, which is a question not just of *what* is filmed, but also a formal question of *how*.

On Dimensionality

In the figure of the sinkhole the horizontal plane of territorial politics and human habitation, and the vertical plane of geological materiality and resource capitalism, collapse into each other. The sinkhole presents a compelling prism for a filmic investigation of the porous contact zone between the human and the geological, as it embodies the intersection of the dynamics of colonialism and territorial volume, infrastructural violence and environmental violence, historical time and deep time, horizontal and vertical planes, looking across a terrain and cutting through it. In the making of *Salarium* the key formal question was around how to depict the continuity of surface and depth, and the interlocked human and geological agencies forming the landscape. Prior to moving on to a discussion of the specific formal approaches that were employed in the making of the film in the next part of the chapter, it is important to pause on the relationship between the moving image medium and visual regimes that have rendered space as flat and quantifiable, while presenting the environment as standing reserve.

Cartography was a large part of the visuality, understood in Mirzoeff's terms as the 'visualization of history' that 'sought to present authority as self-evident' (2011, 2-3), of settler colonialism. These legacies reverberate in the settler colonial project in the West Bank, where Israeli mineral industries profit from divorcing the political control of the surface of the territory from the economic control of the resources underneath. In trying to devise a visual approach for a filmic engagement with this landscape, an approach that aims to manifest a different set of relations between occupants/occupiers and territory, surface and depth, human and nonhuman, life and nonlife, this is the visuality to counter. To develop the formal language of *Salarium*, it is thus crucial to understand how these modes of the dimensional translation of the material world into a flat image operate, how their legacies manifest in film and, only then, how the film medium might be deployed to offer an alternative approach.

Maps represent the surface of a territory – so far so obvious. Unlike images such as paintings and photographs, which, as will be elaborated below, by definition collapse three-dimensional space onto a two-dimensional plane, in depicting the supposedly already two-dimensional surface of the land maps maintain a claim to authority and authenticity in their role as stand-ins for the territory. This is a supposition taken to its extreme by the court cartographers in Jorge Luis Borges's iconic story 'On the Exactitude in Science' (1946), who, in their pursuit to attain a map of perfect accuracy, created a map as big as the territory. Accuracy here is implied to be the domain purely of scale and detail, implying that the map and the territory have a difference merely in degree and not kind. This is the frame of mind that translates into seeing the territory itself as mere surface, with the attendant possibility for a misappropriation of underground resources, as is the case in the West Bank. Even maps that meticulously chart the height of mountains and the depth of valleys represent just the *shape of the surface* and not the volume underneath. Maps also necessarily imply the viewer's position to be that of the God's eye view, obfuscating the potential material realities of the observer's fleshy embodied presence in the three-dimensional environment.

In the opening paragraphs of his key study of the relationship between cartography and cinema, *Cartographic Cinema,* Tom Conley plainly states that 'a film *is* a map' (2007, 5). This is an intriguing premise that can be interpreted in a number of ways that do not necessarily need to imply the visual culture of imperialism. Conley, however, chooses the word 'colonise' as he continues by saying that 'a film can be understood in a broad sense to be a "map"' insofar as it 'colonizes the imagination of the public it is said to ... seek to control' and 'encourages its public to think of the world in concert with its own articulation of space' (1). Perhaps the rigidity in Conley's use of 'colonise' and 'control' as ways to describe the spectatorial experience stems from the fact that his study is focused on the appearance of literal maps in narrative cinema, and he thus conceives of space in the cartographic sense of geography and location. Film's ability to generate an array of different articulations of space, including those impossible anywhere other than in the medium of film, is, I would argue, precisely where it has capacity to set its audience *free*. Classic continuity editing and cinematography techniques such as the 30-degree rule and the 180-degree rule attempt to suppress this aspect of the medium's capacity in order to generate an experience that is continuous with the hegemonic experience of three-dimensional space. Film *can*, however, and often does, produce arrangements of space (and time) heretofore unimaginable. It thus gives the audience tools to imagine, and perhaps enact, alternative arrangements of material space. Geological filmmaking seeks to develop this inherent potential of the medium to manifest new arrangements of space and time by shooting and arranging shots in ways that are not beholden to a desire to faithfully reproduce a likeness of the existing world.

Without Renaissance innovations such as the telescope and advanced cartographic techniques, the practical possibilities for the navigation of oceans and the mapping, quantifying, subdividing and colonising of new territories would have been unthinkable. At the same time, also in the field of optics the invention of linear perspective further enabled the conceptualisation of space as abstractly geometrical and quantifiable. Linear perspective transformed the possibilities of the dimensional conversion of three-dimensional space into a two-dimensional image. Crucially, it was understood not as a technique that was developed, but as an objective property of space that was discovered. A painting made by employing the rules of linear perspective was thus imbued with a claim to objectivity and realism. This claim, however, was not neutral: the claim to objectivity took a pictorial representation of space, the perspectival lines of which converged in a single eye of an ideal viewer, who acted 'as the static centre of the visible world', and then presented 'this view as universally valid by claiming for it the status of reality' (Cosgrove 1998, 22-26). Perspective imbued pictorial depictions of the physical world with supposed objectivity and simultaneously turned them, and, by extension, the physical world they claimed to represent, into objects placed under the control and ownership of individual human subjects.

Both maps and perspectival painting are indebted to, as well as instrumental in, constructing a representationalist worldview that presupposes a separation between representations, entities represented and the knowing/viewing/representing human subject. The task of geological filmmaking becomes to find ways to disrupt a centuries-long history of visual representation that neglects the depth of the landscape, positions it as a prospect ready for subjugation and implies the convergence of things seen in the eye of an ideal observer who remains external to the environment. Or, to state it in the affirmative: the task of geological filmmaking is to develop tools for a situated and embodied image making that positions both image maker and image viewer as part of the environment, that accounts for the volume of the terrain and that presents the landscape as emergent through agencies which are both human and geologic.

Photographic and cinematic capture is generally regarded within the trajectory of perspectival image making. The emergence of both linear perspective and photography have a common ancestor in the camera obscura. Yet a closer attention paid to the material aspect of the translation of three dimensions into two in cinematic capture may provide some tools for working towards undoing perspectivalism. Importantly, unlike perspectival images that converge in a zero-dimensional single point in the eye of an ideal observer, photographic and cinematic images are formed when light reflected off objects in the three-dimensional environment hits the two-dimensional plane of photosensitive material. This plane in fact has a depth of its own – and much has been made of the materiality and chemistry of photographic and cinematic capture, and the organic and inorganic materials entangled in it – from flammable silver nitrate to animal gelatine present in the celluloid (Knowles 2020).

Not only the chemistry but also the physics of cinematic capture is fundamentally different from perspectival depiction, as its mode of dimensional translation is closer to that of a shadow. A shadow is a volumetric phenomenon, formed when a three-dimensional object blocks a portion of light rays, and visually actualised upon a two-dimensional surface that cuts across it. So a photographic or cinematic image is created when the light reflected off three-dimensional objects is chemically actualised on a photosensitive surface that cuts across it. In a process that is continuous with cinematic and photographic capture, cinematic projection takes place when a two-dimensional projection surface cuts through a volume of projected light to actualise its potentiality as image. In geological filmmaking, one potential avenue for generating cinematic alternatives to the perspectival visuality would be through emphasising the photosensitive element of the camera as a material plane intervening in the three-dimensional environment and emphasising projection as volumetric.

In the specific context of making *Salarium*, a key strategy for mobilising the above potentialities of the film medium to subvert and transcend the visuality of settler colonialism was to try to imagine and manifest what a *sinkhole image*, as distinct from a representational image *of* a sinkhole, might look like. A key point is that I do not claim that the sinkhole image does, or aims to, have some privileged access to capturing the 'essence' of the sinkholes, whatever that may mean. Rather, in following the formal cues set up by theorising the sinkholes themselves – surface and depth, life and nonlife, presence and absence, human and non-human agency – through the sinkhole image I aim to develop some tools to address the aesthetic challenges pertaining to the depiction of naturecultural environments more broadly.

The Sinkhole Image

As the landscape by the Dead Sea shore becomes a nexus of the intersection of politics and materiality, infrastructural violence and environmental violence, and horizontal and vertical planes, in our use of the camera we attempted to visually interact with each element on its own terms. We shot the infrastructural elements of the landscape from a tripod with a wide lens, aiming to visually echo the quantifying approach to the space of the cartographic imagination and to thus position seemingly innocuous entities such as roads, orchards and electric pylons as tools of the occupation (fig. 11). When sequenced in the final cut of the film, these static, stable and wide shots gradually weave together a sense of coherent horizontal spatiality. In the environment itself, sinkholes appear as interventions in this horizontality and surface stability. Throughout the film, we aimed to make perceptual and visceral interventions into the stability of the landscape shots to open them up to questions of dimensionality and destabilised depths. Though images *of* sinkholes do appear towards the end of the film, we primarily worked on creating destabilising stylistic interruptions through camera work.

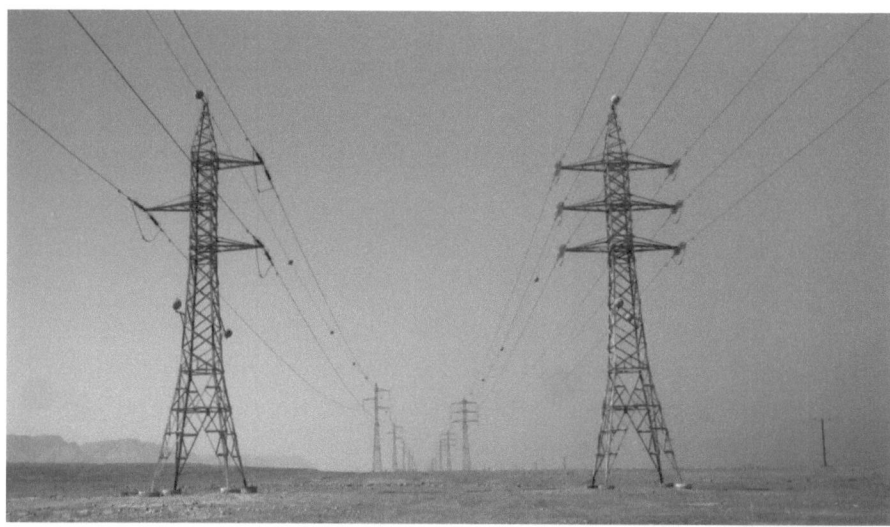
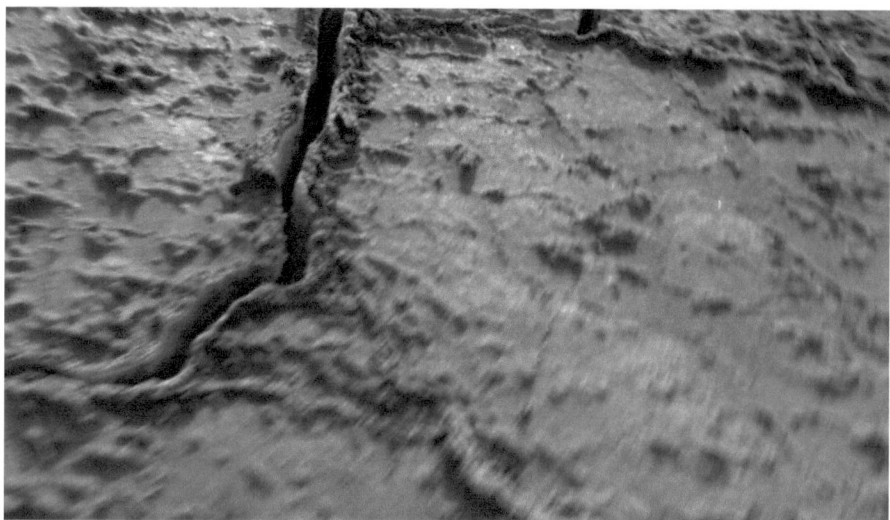

Fig 11. and Fig. 12. Stills from *Salarium* (2017), Sasha Litvintseva and Daniel Mann.

Depiction: Sinkholes

The key camera strategy in disrupting surface stability involved various ways of removing the camera from the stable ground and into the embodied proximity of its occupants. All the images shot on the shores perforated by sinkholes are handheld. As I follow the geologist Eli Raz around the rim of the sinkholes, guiding the camera across the landscape through the motion of my body, the (in)stability of the shots is mediated through the (in)stability of my arms and my steps. When the ground itself stops being dependable, the formal language of the film becomes demonstrably probing of the environment. Fear mixed with heat-stricken dizziness generates increasingly abstract, visceral and vertiginous shots of the ground (fig. 12). Here, the certainty of scale, the continuity of location and a sense of the horizon are replaced with the detail of the geological formations and patterns of salt, mud and rock. As we lose the horizon we lose perspective – and the shots revel in a tactile encounter with the materially abundant world. In another scene the camera is tossed from one person to another. Initially designed as a way to experiment with generating the sensation of falling, the camera's centre of gravity was such that it made it flip on itself with incredible speed – less the sensation of dropping from height than a disintegration of the difference between the above and the below.

We shoot some scenes with (non)actors dressed as soldiers, who had also once been soldiers themselves, applying the mineral mud to their bodies and faces. They perform as agents of the state violence responsible

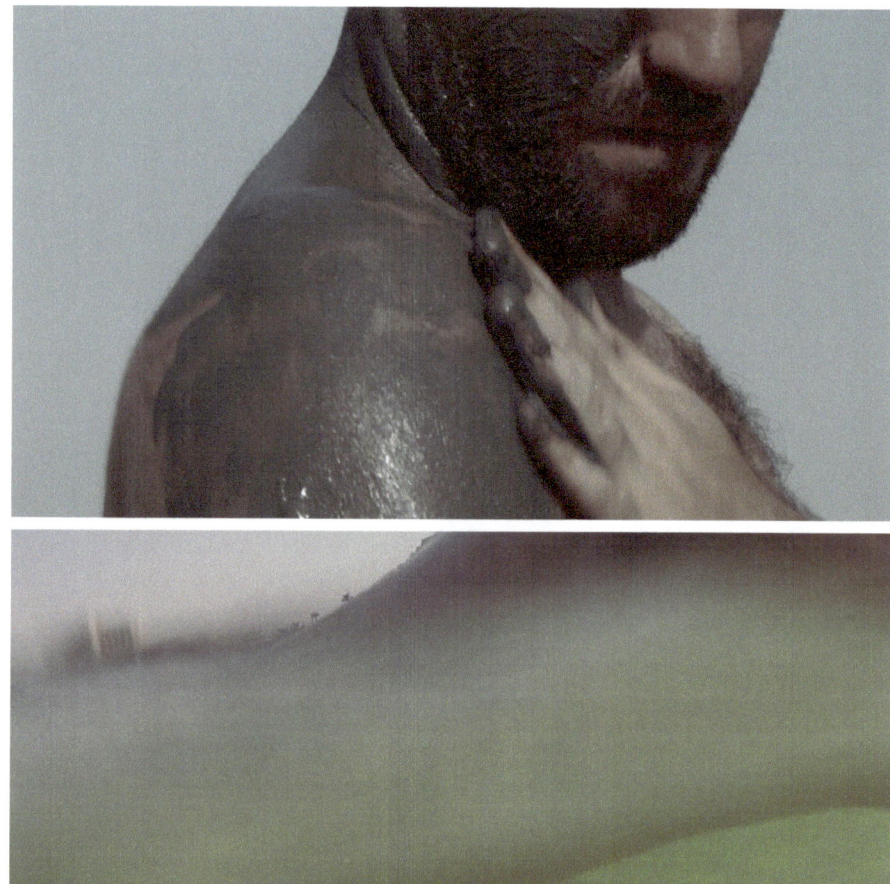

Fig 13. and Fig. 14. Stills from *Salarium* (2017), Sasha Litvintseva and Daniel Mann.

for the confiscation and instrumentalisation of the land, as they wear the material soil on their skin as a token of the militarised territory. Some shots are extreme close-ups of the mud absorbing into the actor-soldiers' skin, as their skin becomes a porous threshold between life and nonlife in defiance of their role as agents of geontopower (or guardians of the distinction of life and nonlife), as well as of classic biopower (fig. 13). As they submerge in the Dead Sea, I follow them into the hot and salty water with the camera. I guide the camera around their floating bodies, their weight supported by the salinity of the water, in extreme proximity. For these shots I use an underwater camera in order to be able to continuously break the surface of the water. Emerging and submerging the camera I aim to generate a sense of the vertical dimension of the landscape, the above and the below, and the permeable nature of the surface that separates them. The water, which due to its salinity is more dependably able to support the weight of a body than the perforated shore, here becomes the horizontal surface of the landscape. Where perspectival images optically represent three-dimensional space as though by providing an immaterial window onto it, the camera movement in this scene positions the lens, and, by extension, the screen, as a material surface that cuts across the three-dimensional environment, as it cuts across the horizontal surface of the water. In cutting the landscape vertically, the camera movement aims to render the surface of the water as perpendicular to the surface of the image, as is particularly evident in the moments where both the above and the below are visible at once (fig. 14). Understanding the image as being on a perpendicular axis to the surface of the landscape creates depth and dimensionality in a way that is very different to that of perspectival images. In thus positioning the image as the outer surface of the landscape, this scene generates a membrane that the sinkhole image seeks to breach.

What is it exactly that breaches a surface? In effect – what is a hole? As Roberto Casati and Achille C. Varzi write in their study of the ontology of holes, a hole in the wall is 'not made of the shadow you see', nor 'of the air that is inside it, nor of the plaster and bits of paint that have fallen on the floor' (1994, 9). A hole, rather, is a superficial phenomenon, meaning it is an interruption in the surface of an otherwise continuous object. Surface is understood here as 'the first part of a material object to come into contact with the object's environment' (11), rather like the skin that separates and links an organism to its environment. An appearance of a hole presupposes the existence of a surface that can be breached, reconfiguring the relationship of inside/outside. In this way, 'holes are parasitic on their hosts' (16). A hole is neither a location nor a presence. 'It is uncertain whether the hole really *occupies* the place where it is localised. In fact, it seems that there is a hole there just *insofar* as nothing occupies that place' (9). A hole, then, is an active *presence of an absence*. A sinkhole, in turn, is not merely an absence in the surface of the ground. It is an active presence of an absence of a portion of the membrane that delineates an inhabitant from their environment, a refusal of the surface that separates life and nonlife.

Film as a medium is uniquely badly placed to portray absence – every image is a presencing of the things depicted, not a negation of those that remain outside the frame. Maya Deren makes this point in comparing film to writing through the opening sentences from Franz Kafka's *The Trial*: 'Someone must have been telling lies about Joseph K. for without having done anything wrong he was arrested one fine morning. His landlady's cook, who always brought his breakfast at eight o'clock, failed to appear on this occasion' (Kafka quoted in Deren 1946, 41). She goes on to argue that it would be nearly impossible to translate the 'failed to appear' into film, as that mere absence would not necessarily be interpreted as *the presence of absence*, an actively 'negative reference' (41). An absencing, however, does present an opportunity to challenge representationalism head on: you would be hard pressed to enact representationalism without the object of representation. It thus presents a crucial practical challenge to explore in the filmmaking.

Almost exactly halfway, *Salarium* is punctuated by a narrated story of the experience of being swallowed by a sinkhole. In seeking the most appropriate visual component for this part of the film, we came to the realisation that perhaps the sinkhole image that punctuates the visual landscape of the film is no image at all – it is an active presence of an absence. As Eli Raz tells of his experience of bodily vulnerability and the loss of agency as a result of the agency of the sinkhole that swallowed him, the screen remains black. This is not to say that the ticket out of the representationalist bind is to make no images at all. Should that have indeed been the case, this chapter would not have proceeded beyond the first paragraphs. Crucially, the absence of image in this instance is *presenced* by the images that surround it. They are what gives its absence a duration and their content is what gives it meaning. A durational lack of image is thus not the same as a lack of images altogether – it is a presencing of time. And the presencing of time is something that film is indeed uniquely well-placed to do. In this instance the sinkhole image punctures the film temporally: the linear duration of the film is the surface that is breached by it and thus given depth.

Where sinkholes disrupt infrastructure, such as roads and agricultural fields, and thus make it visible, the absent sinkhole image makes visible the infrastructure of the film's screening. In this moment of being confronted with the affective dimension of being consumed by a sinkhole, we are left with the material specificities of the circumstances of our watching: these too constitute the depth of the image. While the screen remains black, it does not read merely as absence, as nothing, but rather it presences the projection surface (or LED screen) as a material and spatial phenomenon onto itself. The sudden disappearance of a figurative image on screen draws attention to the screen itself. As Giuliana Bruno poetically elucidates in *Surface*, the surface of cinematic projection 'is not superficial but is a substantial plane of relational transformation that has texture and depth', as the phenomenon of projection itself reveals 'the thickness of surface' (2014, 108). She writes that by focusing on 'the actual fabric of the screen, outside of figuration' (3), the projection surface 'far from representing any perspectival ideal, is no longer containable within optical framings, and cannot be likened to a window or a mirror' (5). The presencing of the screen as a material thickness presents an alternative to perspectivalism. It also presents an avenue towards reanimating the depth and dimensionality of cinematic images and, with that, the depth and dimensionality of the landscapes they depict. A consideration of the material specificity of the film experience thus becomes an integral part of the work of depicting environments beyond what is visible on their surface.

The material specificity of the shooting experience also lurks behind the surface of each image. Every image in the film is precisely what it is as a result of the circumstances under which it was shot. Industrial fiction film production bends environments to its will: the image pre-exists its own making and dictates the transformation of the material world towards its needs. The type of filmmaking I analyse in this book is first and foremost about attentiveness to the specificities of environments as they are: images arise out of the material circumstances. Of course one cannot help but bring preconceived ideas, but one also has to confront that there is only so much that is physically possible – and this is precisely the point: to be responsive and responsible toward the physical limitations of the environment. As recounted in the opening to this book, the extreme heat meant that most of the shooting had to happen in ninety-second intervals between air-conditioning breaks. This material constraint meant adapting my shooting style to committing to a single shot of any given scene, instead of gathering multiple angles, thus creating images that have to contain the wealth and depth of detail simultaneously. Alternatively, it meant spending a substantial amount of time in a given location, a time in which things would shift and characters – soldiers and prophets, settlers and tourists – come and go, all of which would make it into the film, adding layers of depth to the hostile landscape through seeing who chooses, is forced or is allowed to be there. The temporality of the film – indeed, the duration of every shot beyond its metric duration – thus includes the ninety seconds during which the camera can stand the heat of the sun.

These added non-linear layers of the film's duration have potentially far-reaching implications. As Jason W. Moore argues, the Western conceptions of 'nature as external, space as flat and geometrical, and time as linear' are all mutually reinforcing and share their historical and political origins (2015, 191). Alongside developing methods for destabilising the apprehension of space as flat by engaging with the depth of the image, the filmmaking process was also about questioning what the depth of time might mean as an alternative to linearity. The temporality of the sinkholes themselves is anything but linear and unfolds on a number of scales. Sinkholes are the result of the millions-of-years-long history of the underground salt deposits on the Dead Sea shore as much as of the decades-long history of colonial settlement, mineral extraction and desert irrigation. But sinkholes do not merely combine these two temporal scales: they intervene. In appearing, they disrupt the possibility of a linear progression of either topsoil sedimenting on the salt deposits or the continued capitalisation of the land through extraction and cultivation. In this sense, more than operating on multiple scales, sinkholes embody multiple modes of relating to the past and the future. On the one hand, time as it is experienced when traversing the perforated landscape is of an intense anticipation of the sudden forming of a new sinkhole: the now of this anticipation already contains the potential future collapse. When a sinkhole does appear, the pressure valve of the present is released and the preceding breadth of time flows in: the entirety of the past that has made the sinkhole possible is made present in it. In both cases the temporality of the sinkhole is not the chronological or teleological time of one-thing-after-another, but of an expansive present opening up towards the future, and of the expanse of the deep past made manifest at once.

The time of the sinkhole unfolds according to what Barad calls the 'sedimenting process of becoming', a material temporality where 'the past matters and so does the future, but the past is never left behind, never finished once and for all, and the future is not what will come to be in an unfolding of the present moment; rather the past and the future are enfolded participants in matter's iterative becoming' (Barad 2007, 181). In a material concept of time such as this, both the past and the future are already inscribed in the present. Sinkholes simultaneously contain the ongoing geological and anthropogenic processes that have resulted in the contemporary devastation of the landscape, its current conditions, as well as the anticipation of future change that has already been set in motion. The temporality of the Dead Sea landscape, as it is transforming through the influence of both anthropogenic and geologic forces, can also be read through what Astrida Neimanis and Rachel Loewen Walker (2014) call ecological thick time: a temporality that is woven together by both human and nonhuman actors, actions and durations. Thick time is also a material temporality that 'understands that matter has a memory of the past, and this memory swells as it creates and unmakes possible futures' (Neimanis and Lowen Walker 2014, 570). The thickness of time simultaneously and nonchronologically contains not only the past, present and future, but also a multiplicity of parallel and interacting human and nonhuman durations. In the case of the landscape surrounding the Dead Sea, these durations range from the time it took the salt deposits to form in the subterrain and the time it takes the salt to melt, to the length of the Israeli occupation of the West Bank and the time it takes an artificially irrigated date grove to bloom

– all of these durations coalesce in the thick time of the sinkhole.

In the methodology of geological filmmaking, the act of engaging with a particular nonhuman entity through practical filmmaking becomes a means by which to learn more about the qualities of this entity and the way it intersects with human systems and processes. This methodology also provided insights that are more broadly applicable to conceiving of and engaging with the ecological crisis. But, equally importantly, the detailed engagement with the nonhuman subject of the film becomes a prism through which to discover new ways of thinking about the medium of film itself. Here, conceptualising the non-linear thick time of the sinkhole became an entry point to a new way of thinking of cinematic temporality ecologically as the *depth* of time.

As discussed in the 'Grounding' chapter, film duration is already multidimensional. Within it coalesce the past time of the process of the film's making and the deep past of the formation of the geological materials that make up cinematic technologies, as well as the future tense of all its potential screenings and the deep future of the materiality of the hardware. Alongside all of these durations, each image in *Salarium* contains the durations of the time of production, including the ninety-second intervals in which the shots are made, and the human and nonhuman durations congealed in the production of the sinkholes themselves. The thickness, or, in other words, *depth*, of cinematic time can be understood as containing the durations of all the human and nonhuman processes that coalesce to bring the image into being. The depth of time here refers not to the time that is most distant to the present moment, which is ordinarily called geological 'deep time', but rather to the depth and thickness of the temporal and material relations of the present moment itself, which I call *the deep now*. In considering all the very concrete environmental, political, social, technological and material factors that make the cinematic image possible and bring it into being, we must also consider all the environmental, political, social, technological and material factors that bring into being each profilmic event, location or phenomenon. 'The deep now' further demands that we account for all the human and nonhuman factors that bring *this* present moment into being. A confrontation with geological agency may seem to imply a confrontation with the impossibly incommensurable scale of deep time, but the deep now points to the fact that human agency need only engage with the immediate and proximate ecological dimensionality of *this* present. It thus makes futurity thinkable as it positions the present moment from the perspective of the potential for agency it holds.

What might it mean to imagine the future of geological filmmaking itself? Does it warrant a speculation on what it might mean on a geological timescale? Would these (or indeed any) films still exist in one hundred, one thousand or one hundred thousand years? Projecting the films I made into even the very near future begs the question of how their technical carriers, from hard drives and servers to file formats and playback software, are going to fare with the passage of time. And whether in being subject to entropy they will end up revealing, with a dramatic irony, something that is happening to us now or that awaits us in the future without our knowing, the way the damaged tape communicated the latent material temporality of asbestos. Whatever happens to them, for as long as they persist these films will be a document of *this* moment, a moment in which we will perhaps be seen to have begun to come to grips with our place in the material world, a moment that already contains inscriptions of the coming future. These films were also made *for* this moment: one of many tools for trying to navigate it. Geological filmmaking is therefore of and for the deep now of *right now*. Ultimately, while not too long from now the film files may become unreadable and the films disappear altogether, my hope is that the future of this project will lie in its conceptual and methodological reverberation.

The two films co-directed by Sasha Litvintseva, Asbestos (2016) and Salarium (2017), can be accessed via the book's page on the Open Humanities Press' website.

Works Cited

Alaimo, S. 2010. *Bodily Natures: Science, Environment, and the Material Self.* Bloomington & Indianapolis: Indiana University Press.

Alaimo, S. 2017. 'Your Shell on Acid: Material Immersion, Anthropocene Dissolves'. In R. Grusin, ed. *Anthropocene Feminism.* Minneapolis and London: University of Minnesota Press, 89-120.

Anonymous. 1866. 'Asbestos' in *New York Times (1857–1922)*, August 19. ProQuest Historical Newspapers: *New York Times.*

Anonymous. 1909. 'Paradoxical Asbestos' in *New York Times (1857–1922)*, November 21. ProQuest Historical Newspapers: *New York Times.*

Barad, K. 2007. *Meeting the Universe Halfway: Quantum Physics and the Entanglement of Matter and Meaning.* Durham and London: Duke University Press.

Barad, K. 2012. 'On Touching – The Inhuman That Therefore I Am'. *Differences: A Journal of Feminist Cultural Studies*, 23(3): 206-223.

Bergson, H. 2002. *Henri Bergson: Key Writings*. Eds. K. A. Pearson and J. Mullarkey. New York and London: Continuum.

Bobbette, A. 2013. 'Episodes from a History of Scalelessness: William Jerome Harrison and Geological Photography'. In *Architecture in the Anthropocene: Encounters Among Design, Deep Time, Science and Philosophy*. Ed. E. Turpin. Ann Arbor: Open Humanities Press.

Borges, J. L. 1998 [1946]. 'On the Exactitude in Science'. In *Collected Fictions.* Trans. A. Hurley. London: Penguin Books.

Bruno, G. 2014. *Surface: Matters of Aesthetics, Materiality, and Media*. Chicago and London: University of Chicago Press.

Casati, R. and A. Varzi. 1994. *Holes and Other Superficialities.* Cambridge, MA: MIT Press.

Clark, N. 2017. 'Politics of Strata'. *Theory, Culture & Society*, special issue: Geosocial Formations and the Anthropocene, 34(2-3): 211-231.

Cohen, J. J. 2015. *Stone: An Ecology of the Inhuman*. Minneapolis and London: University of Minnesota Press.

Conley, T. 2007. *Cartographic Cinema*. Minneapolis and London: University of Minnesota Press.

Cosgrove, D. E. 1998. *Social Formation and Symbolic Landscape*. Madison and London: University of Wisconsin Press.

Cubitt, S. 2014. *The Practice of Light: A Genealogy of Visual Technologies from Prints to Pixels*. Cambridge, MA: MIT Press.

Cubitt, S. 2017. *Finite Media: Environmental Implications of Digital Technologies*. Durham and London: Duke University Press.

Daston, L. and P. Galison. 1992. 'The Image of Objectivity'. *Representations*, No. 40, special issue: Seeing Science (Autumn): 81-128.

Deleuze, G. 2005. *Cinema 2: The Time-Image*. Trans. H. Tomlinson and R. Galeta. Minneapolis: University of Minnesota Press.

Deleuze, G. and F. Guattari. 1987. *A Thousand Plateaus: Capitalism and Schizophrenia*. Trans. B. Massumi. Minneapolis and London: University of Minnesota Press.

De Landa, M. 1997. *A Thousand Years of Nonlinear History*. New York: Zone Books.

Demos, T. J. 2017. *Against the Anthropocene: Visual Culture and Environment Today*. Berlin: Sternberg Press.

Deren, M. 1946. *An Anagram of Ideas on Art, Form and Film*. New York: The Alicat Book Shop Press.

Deren, M. 2008. *Essential Deren: Collected Writings on Film*. Ed. B. R. McPherson. Kingston, NY: Documentext.

Doane, M. A. 2002. *The Emergence of Cinematic Time: Modernity, Contingency, the Archive*. Cambridge and London: Harvard University Press.

Dulac, G. 2018. *Writings on Cinema (1919-1937)*. Ed. P. Hillairet. Trans. S. Hammen. Paris: Paris Expérimental.

Elsaesser, T. and M. Hagener. 2015. *Film Theory: An Introduction Through the Senses*. New York and London: Routledge.

Engels, F. 1946 [1883]. *The Dialectics of Nature*. Trans. C. Dutt. London: Lawrence and Wishart, Ltd.

Epstein, J. 1981. 'Bonjour Cinéma and Other Writings by Jean Epstein'. *Afterimage*, 10 (Autumn): 9-38.

Epstein, J. 2012a [1926]. 'The Cinema Seen from Etna'. In *Jean Epstein: Critical Essays and New Translations*. Eds. S. Keller and J. N. Paul. Amsterdam: Amsterdam University Press.

Epstein, J. 2012b [1947]. 'To a Second Reality, a Second Reason'. In *Jean Epstein: Critical Essays and New Translations*. Eds. S. Keller and J. N. Paul. Amsterdam: Amsterdam University Press.

Forrest, A. 2017. 'The Death of Diesel: Has the One-time Wonder Fuel Become the New Asbestos?'. *The Guardian*, April 13, https://www.theguardian.com/cities/2017/apr/13/death-of-diesel-wonder-fuel-new-asbestos

Ghosh, A. 2016. *The Great Derangement: Climate Change and the Unthinkable*. Chicago and London: University of Chicago Press.

Gregson, N., H. Watkins and M. Calestani. 2010. 'Inextinguishable Fibres: Demolition and the Vital Materialisms of Asbestos'. *Environment and Planning A*, vol. 42: 1065-1083.

Haraway, D. 1988. 'Situated Knowledges: The Science Question in Feminism and the Privilege of Partial Perspective'. *Feminist Studies*, 14(3): 575-599.

Heidegger, M. 1995. *The Fundamental Concepts of Metaphysics: World, Finitude, Solitude*. Trans. W. McNeill and N. Walker. Bloomington: Indiana University Press.

Holl, U. 2017. *Cinema, Trace and Cybernetics*. Trans. D. Hendrickson. Amsterdam: Amsterdam University Press.

Ivakhiv, A. J. 2013. *Ecologies of the Moving Image: Cinema, Affect, Nature*. Waterloo, Ontario: Wilfrid Laurier Press.

Jones, R. H. 1888. *Asbestos: Its Production and Use*. London: Crosby Lockwood and Son.

Knowles, K. 2020. *Experimental Film and Photochemical Practices*. London: Palgrave Macmillan.

Lyotard, J.-F. 1991. *The Inhuman: Reflections on Time*. Trans. G. Bennington and R. Bowlby. Stanford: Stanford University Press.

Marks, L. U. 1998. 'Video Haptics and Erotics'. *Screen*, 39(4): 331-348.

Mirzoeff, N. 2011. *The Right to Look: A Counterhistory of Visuality*. Durham: Duke University Press.

Mirzoeff, N. 2013. 'The Climate Crisis is a Debt Crisis'. *The South Atlantic Quarterly*, 112(4): 831-838.

Mirzoeff, N. 2014 'Visualizing the Anthropocene'. *Public Culture*, 26(2): 213-232.

Moore, J. 2015. *Capitalism in the Web of Life: Ecology and the Accumulation of Capital*. London and New York: Verso.

Morton, T. 2016. 'Radiation as Hyperobject'. In *Nuclear Culture Source Book*. Ed. E. Carpenter. London: Black Dog Publishing,165-172.

Nancy, J.-L. 1993. *The Birth to Presence*. Trans. B. Holmes. Stanford: Stanford University Press.

Neimanis, A. 2015. 'No Representation without Colonisation? (Or, Nature Represents Itself)'. *Somatechnics*, 5(2): 135–153.

Neimanis, A. and R. Loewen Walker. 2014. '*Weathering*: Climate Change and the "Thick Time" of Transcorporeality'. *Hypatia*, 29(3): 558-575.

Nixon, R. 2011. *Slow Violence and the Environmentalism of the Poor.* Cambridge and London: Harvard University Press.

Parikka, J. 2012. *What Is Media Archaeology?* Cambridge: Polity.

Parikka, J. 2015. *A Geology of Media.* Minneapolis and London: University of Minnesota Press.

Pliny the Elder. 1855. *Natural History.* Trans. and eds. J. Bostock and H. T. Riley. London: Taylor and Francis.

Povinelli, E. A. 2016. *Geontologies: A Requiem to Late Liberalism.* Durham and London: Duke University Press.

Puig de la Bellacasa, M. 2017. *Matters of Care: Speculative Ethics in More Than Human Worlds.* Minneapolis and London: University of Minnesota Press.

Ruff, K. 2017. 'How Canada Changed from Exporting Asbestos to Banning Asbestos: The Challenges That Had to Be Overcome'. *International Journal of Environmental Research and Public Health.* N. 14, 1135:1-9.

Sartre, J.-P. 1976. *Critique of Dialectical Reason.* Trans. A. Sheridan-Smith. London: HLB, 181–82.

Schuppli, S. 2011. 'Material Malfeasance: Trace Evidence of Violence in Three Image-Acts'. *Photoworks,* 17 (Autumn/Winter): 28-33.

Schuppli, S. 2016. 'Dirty Pictures'. In *Living Earth: Field Notes from the Dark Ecology Project 2014-2016.* Amsterdam: Sonic Acts Press,189-210.

Schuppli, S. 2020. *Material Witness: Media, Forensics, Evidence*. Cambridge, MA: MIT Press.

Sheikh, S. 2018. 'Violence'. In *Posthuman Glossary*. Eds. R. Braidotti and M. Hlavajova. London and New York: Bloomsbury Academic, 449-452.

Shields, F. 2019. 'Why We're Rethinking the Images We Use for Our Climate Journalism', *The Guardian*, October 18, https://www.theguardian.com/environment/2019/oct/18/guardian-climate-pledge-2019-images-pictures-guidelines

Skinner, H. C. W. 2003. 'Mineralogy of Asbestos Minerals'. *Indoor and Built Environ*, 0: 1-5.

Skinner, H. C. W., M. Ross and C. Frondel, C. 1988. *Asbestos and Other Fibrous Materials: Mineralogy, Crystal Chemistry, and Health Effects*. New York and Oxford: Oxford University Press.

Spivak, G. C. 1988. 'Can the Subaltern Speak?'. In *Marxism and the Interpretation of Culture*. Eds. C. Nelson and L. Grossberg. Urbana: University of Illinois Press, 271-313.

Valiaho, P. 2010. *Mapping the Moving Image: Gesture, Thought and Cinema circa 1900*. Amsterdam: Amsterdam University Press.

Van Horssen, J. 2016. *A Town Called Asbestos: Environmental Contamination, Health, and Resilience in a Resource Community*. Vancouver: University of British Columbia Press.

Vogl, J. 2007. 'Becoming-media: Galileo's Telescope'. Trans. B. Hanrahan. *Grey Room,* 29: 14-25.

Weizman, E. 2002. 'The Politics of Verticality'. http://www.opendemocracy.net/ecology-politicsverticality/article_801.jsp

Yusoff, K. 2013. 'Insensible Worlds: Postrelational Ethics, Indeterminacy and the (K)nots of Relating'. *Environment and Planning D: Society and Space,* 31: 208-226.

Yusoff, K. 2018. *A Billion Black Anthropocenes or None.* Minneapolis: University of Minnesota Press.

Zylinska, J. 2018. *Nonhuman Photography.* Cambridge, MA: MIT Press.

www.ingramcontent.com/pod-product-compliance
Lightning Source LLC
Chambersburg PA
CBHW040055250526
45473CB00042B/2417